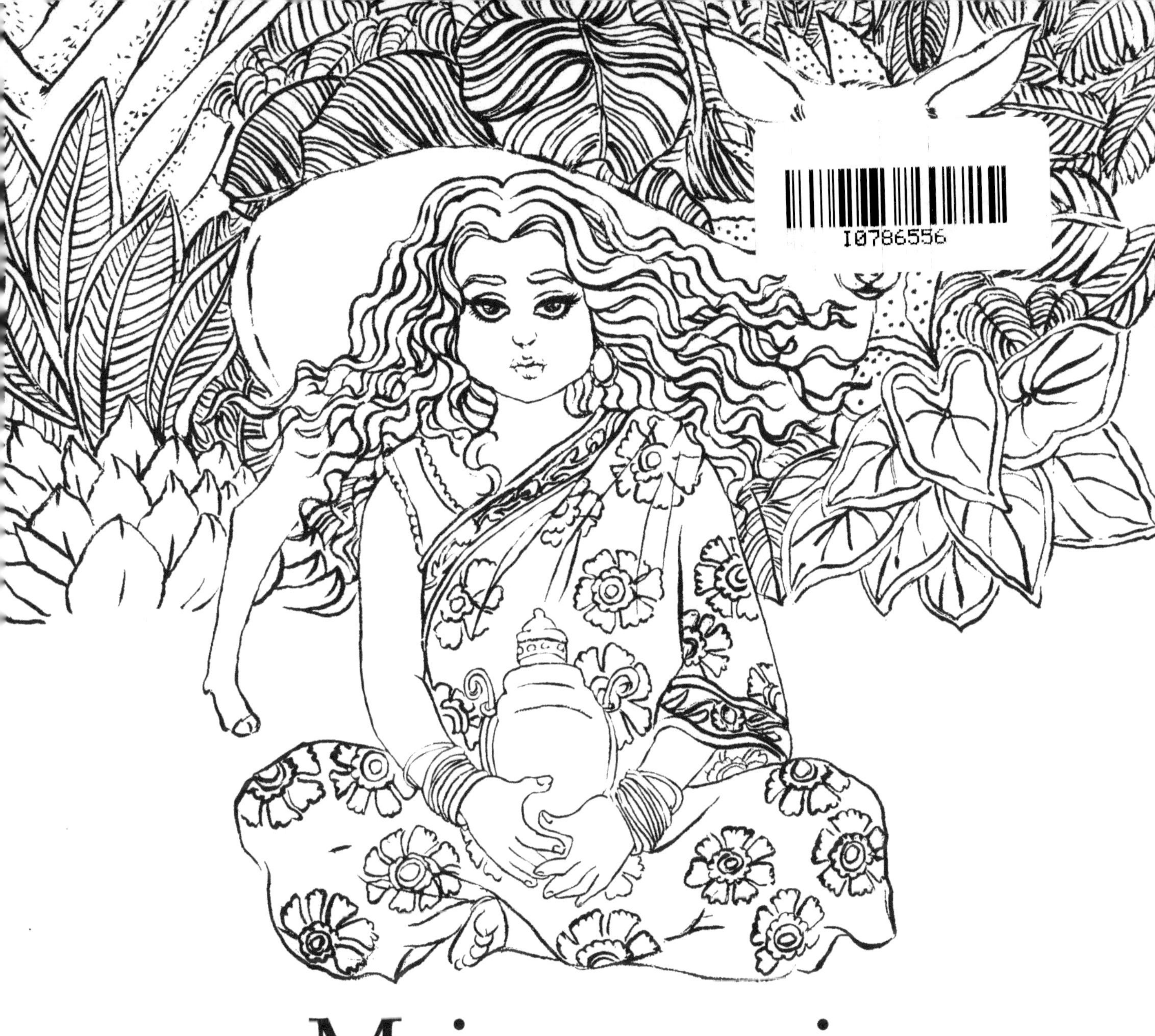

Mrignayani

her deer like eyes

by Jofelyn Martinez Khapra

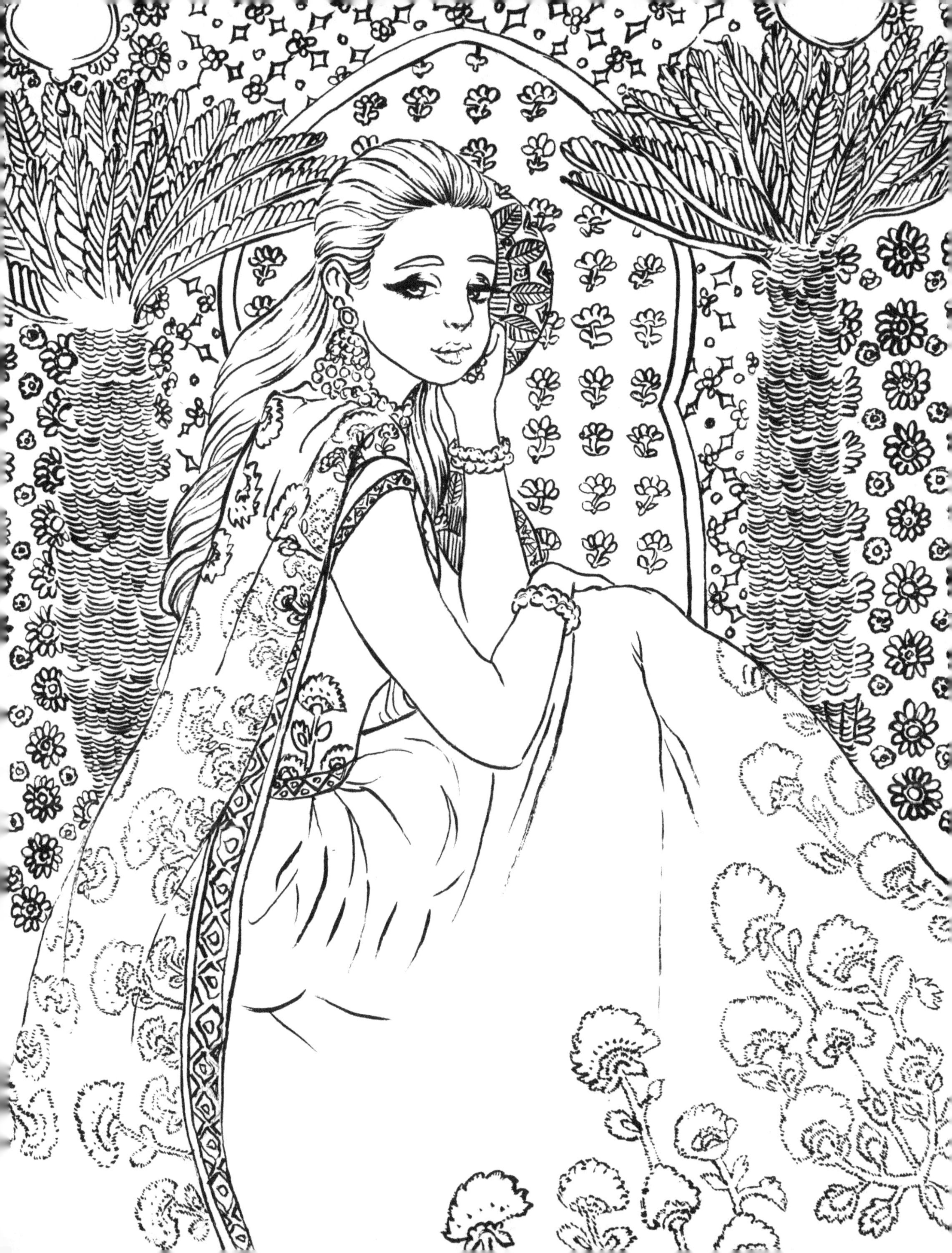

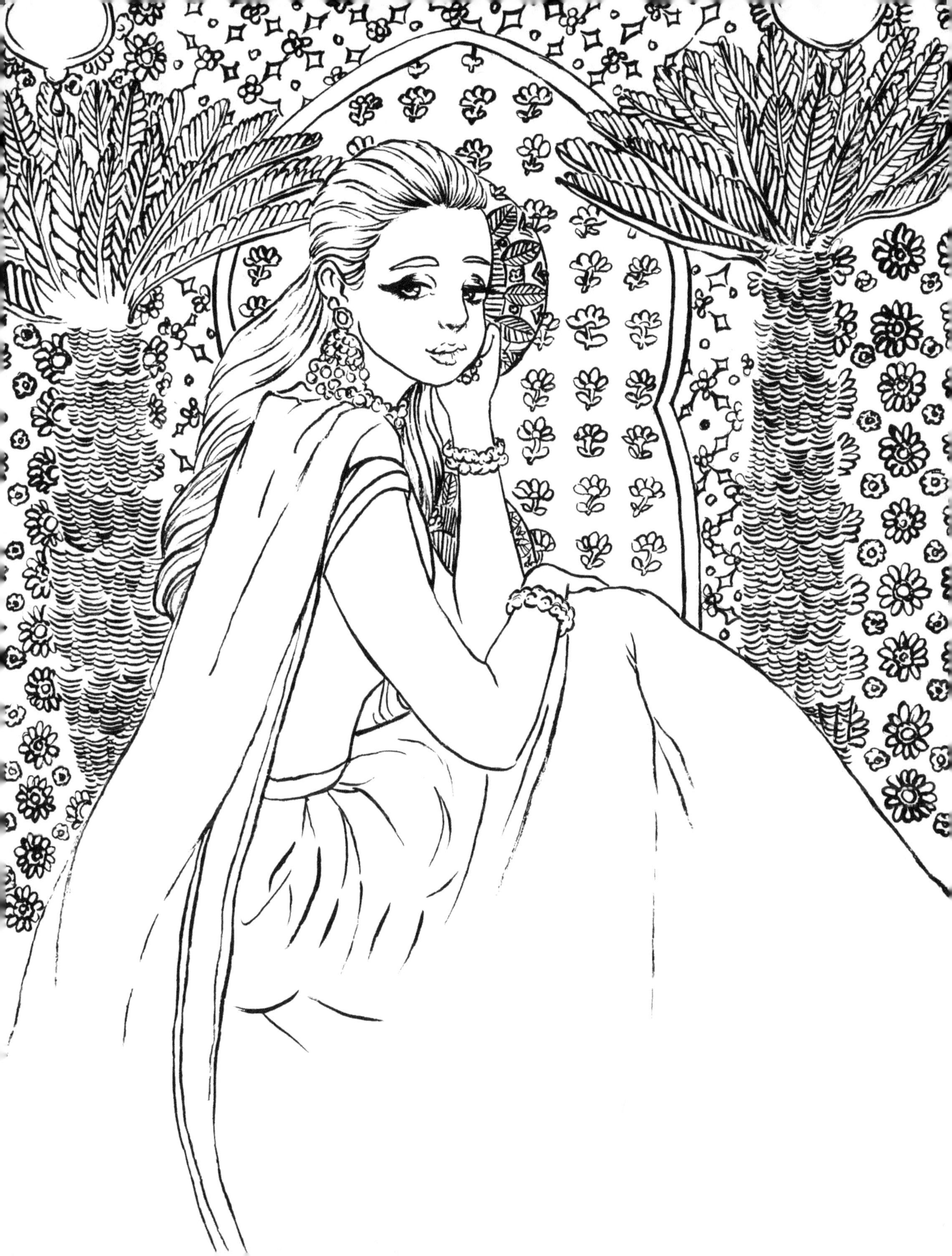

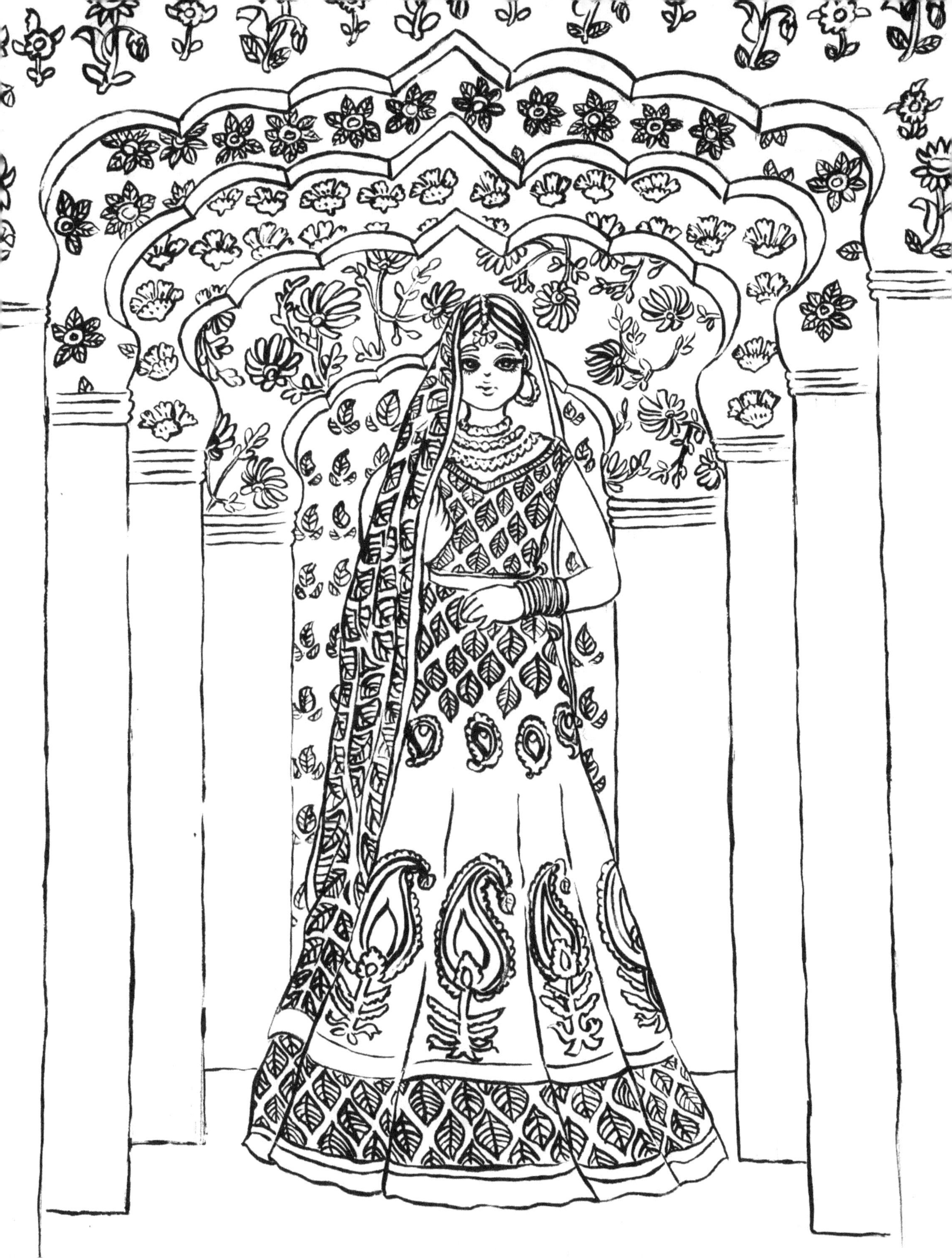

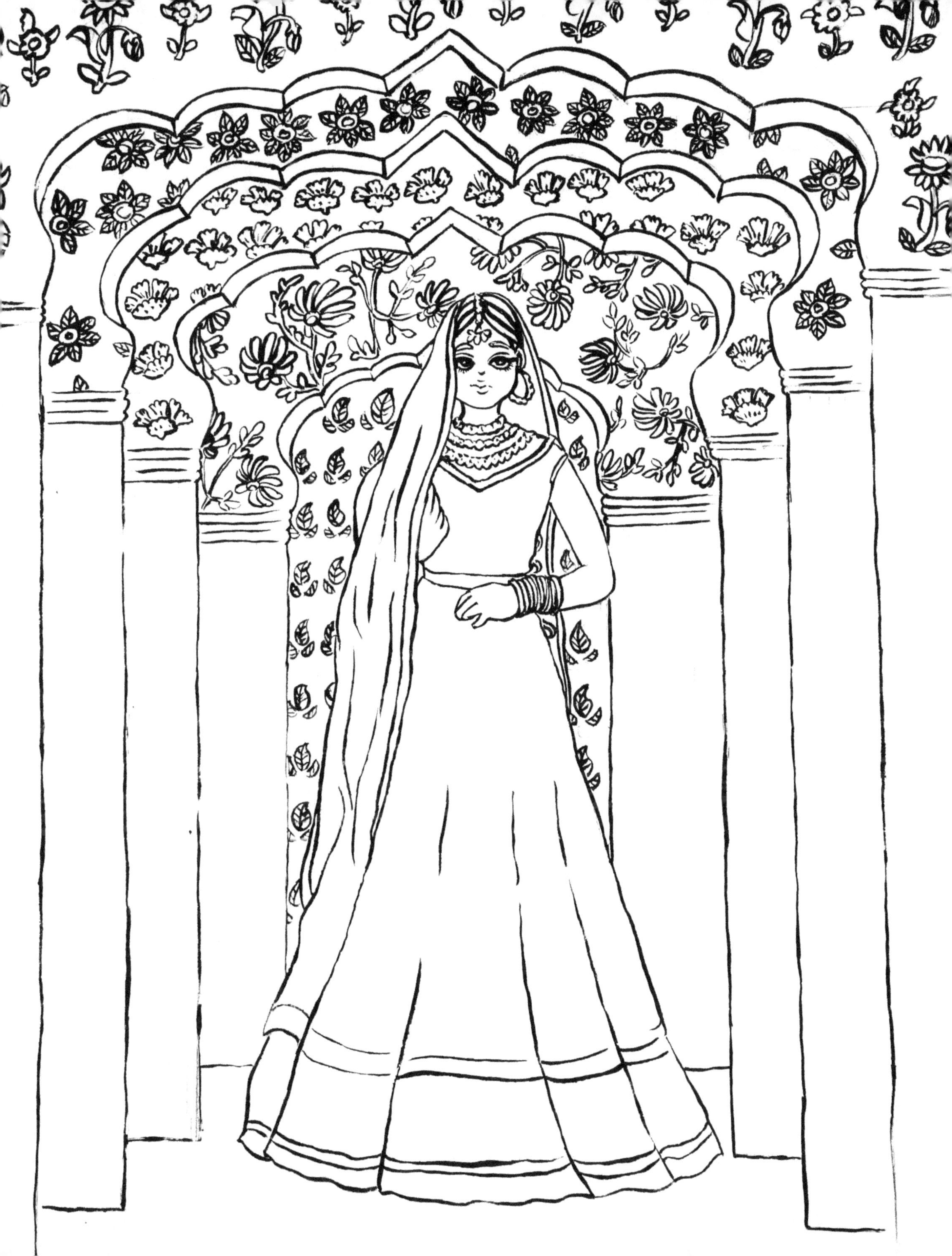

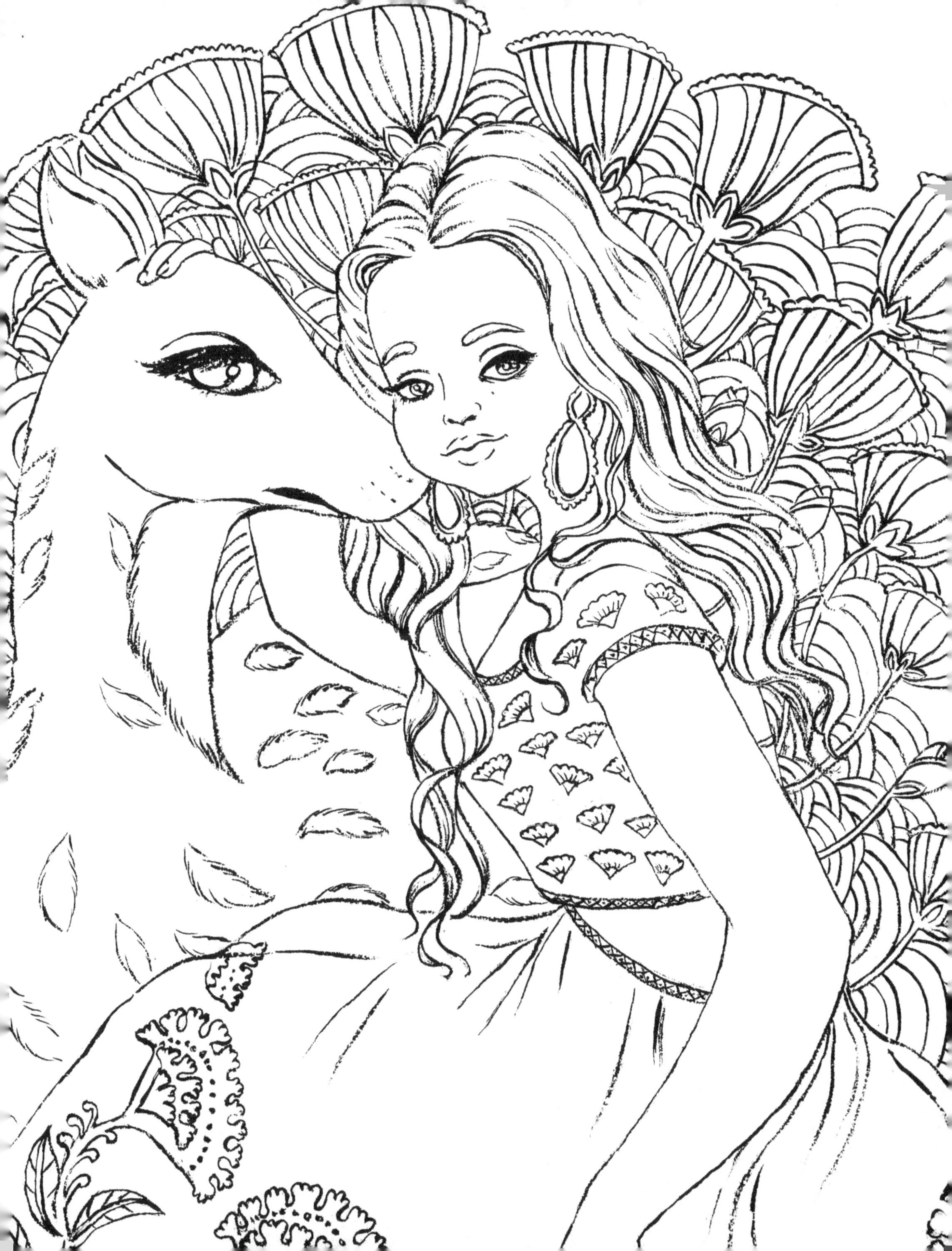

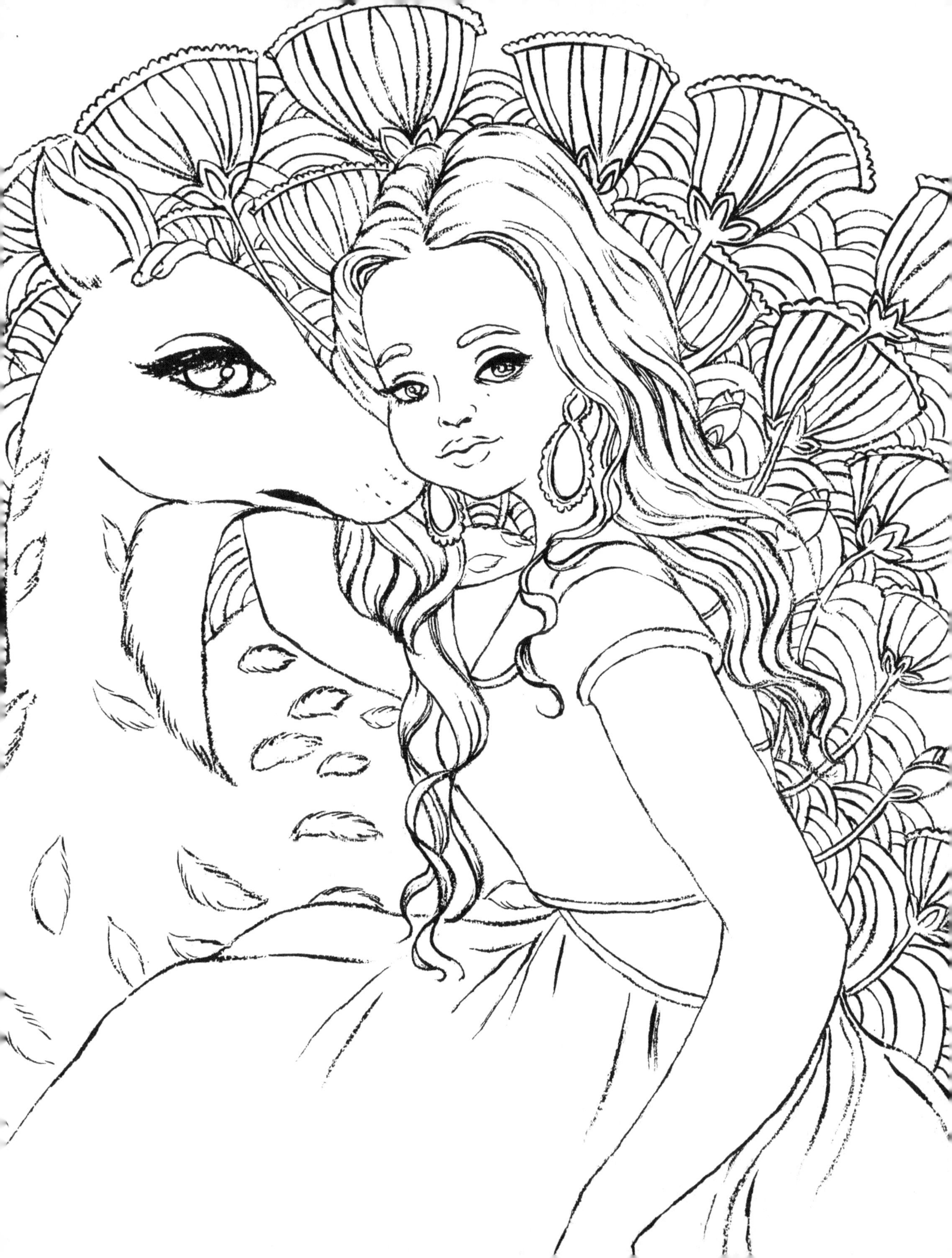

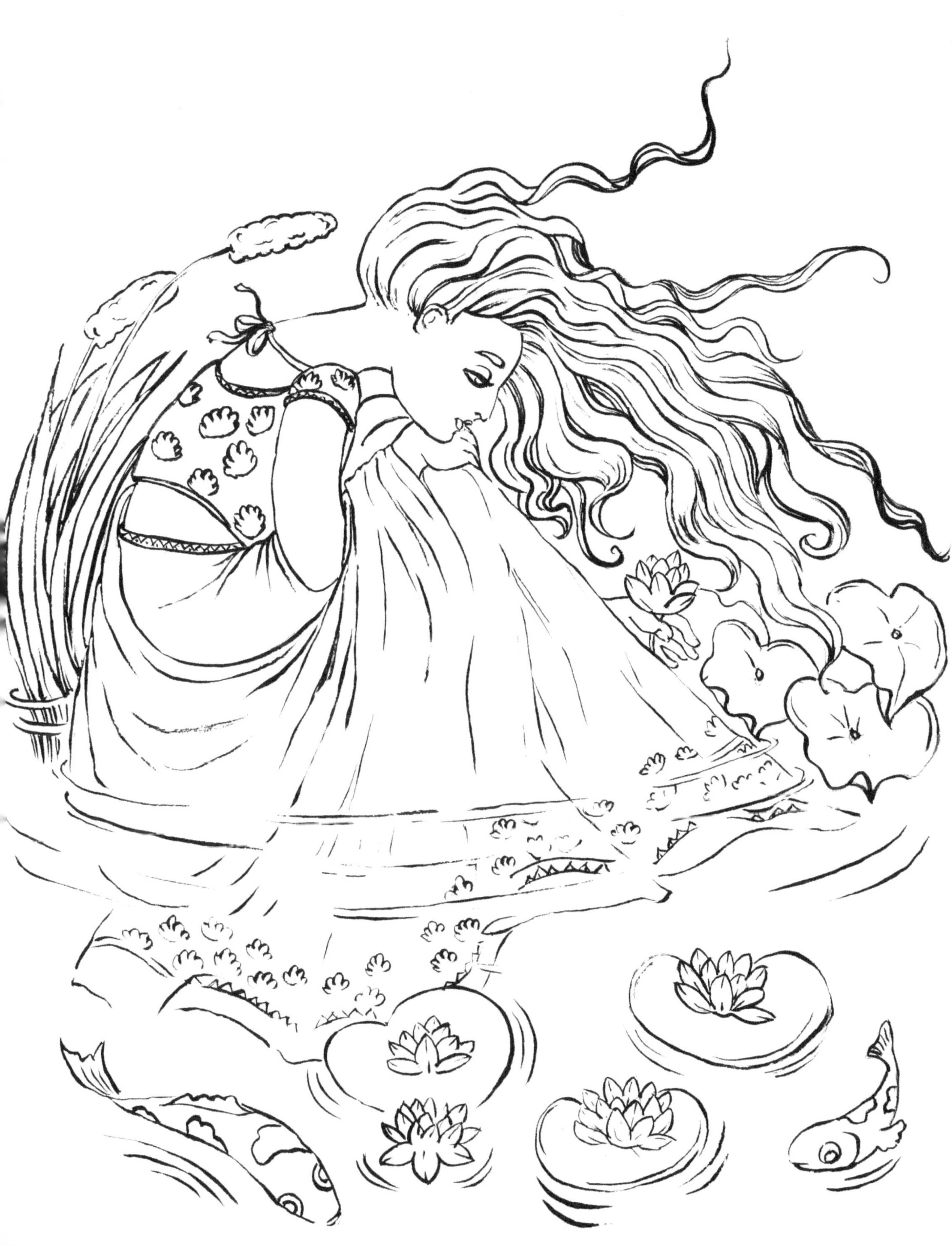

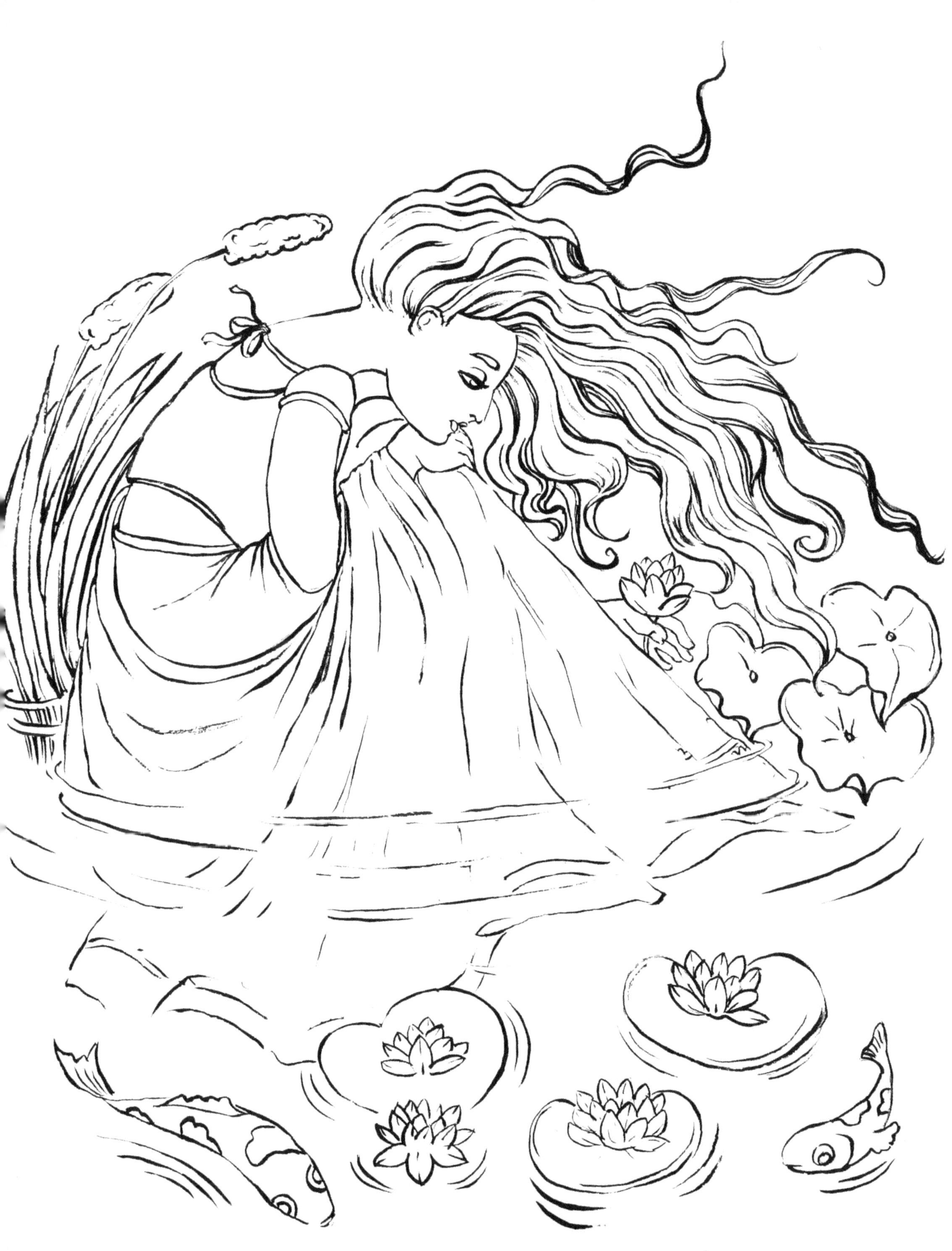

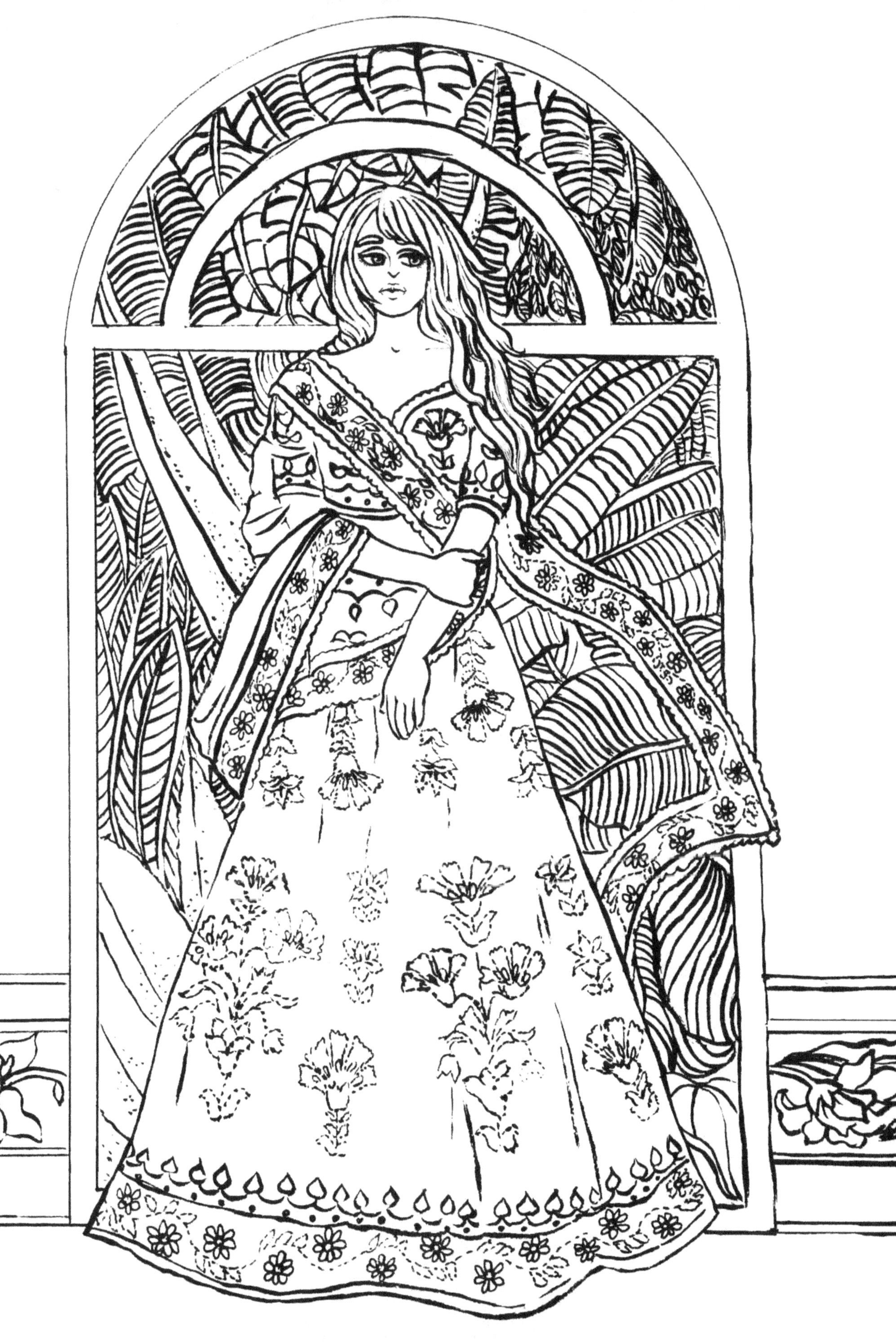

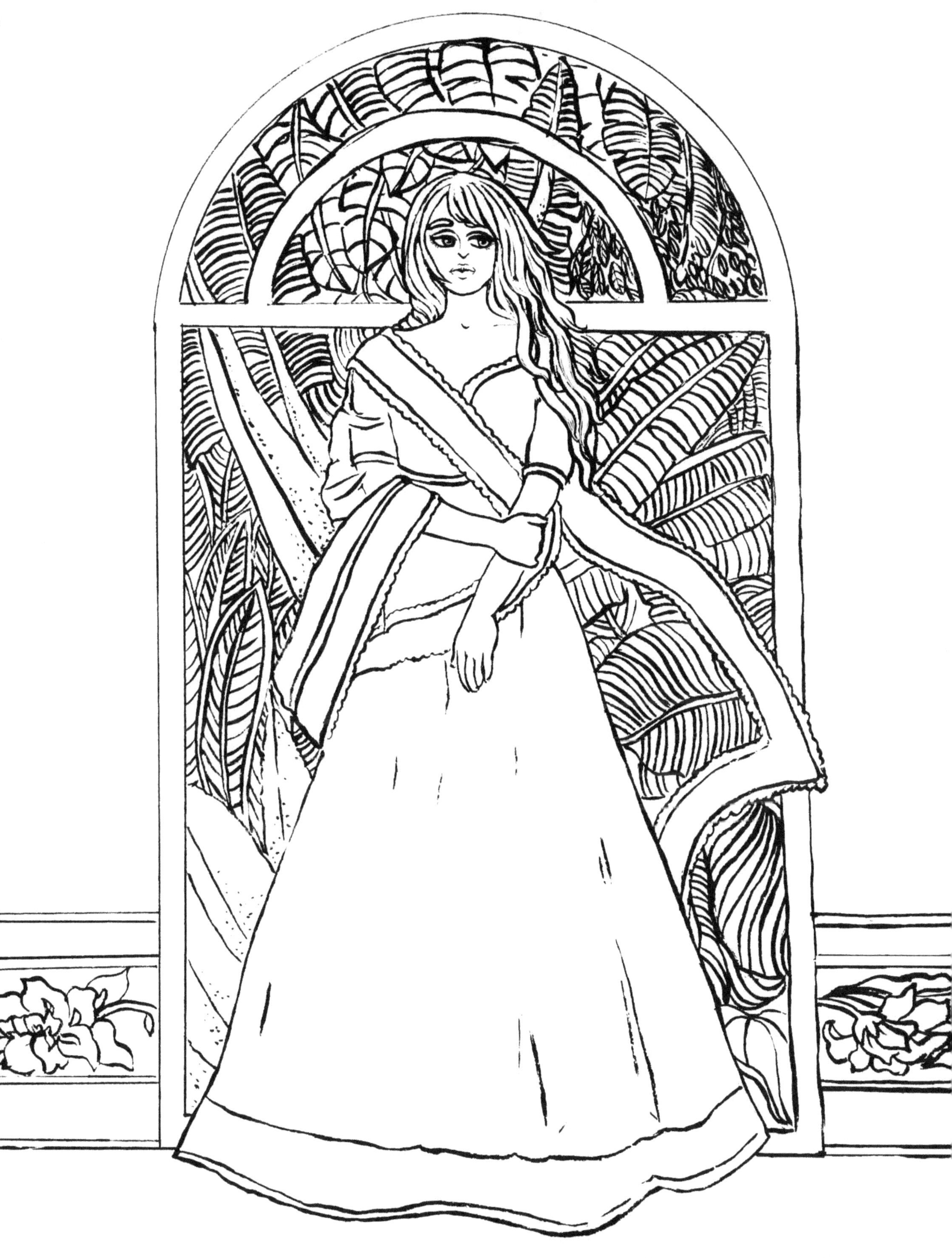

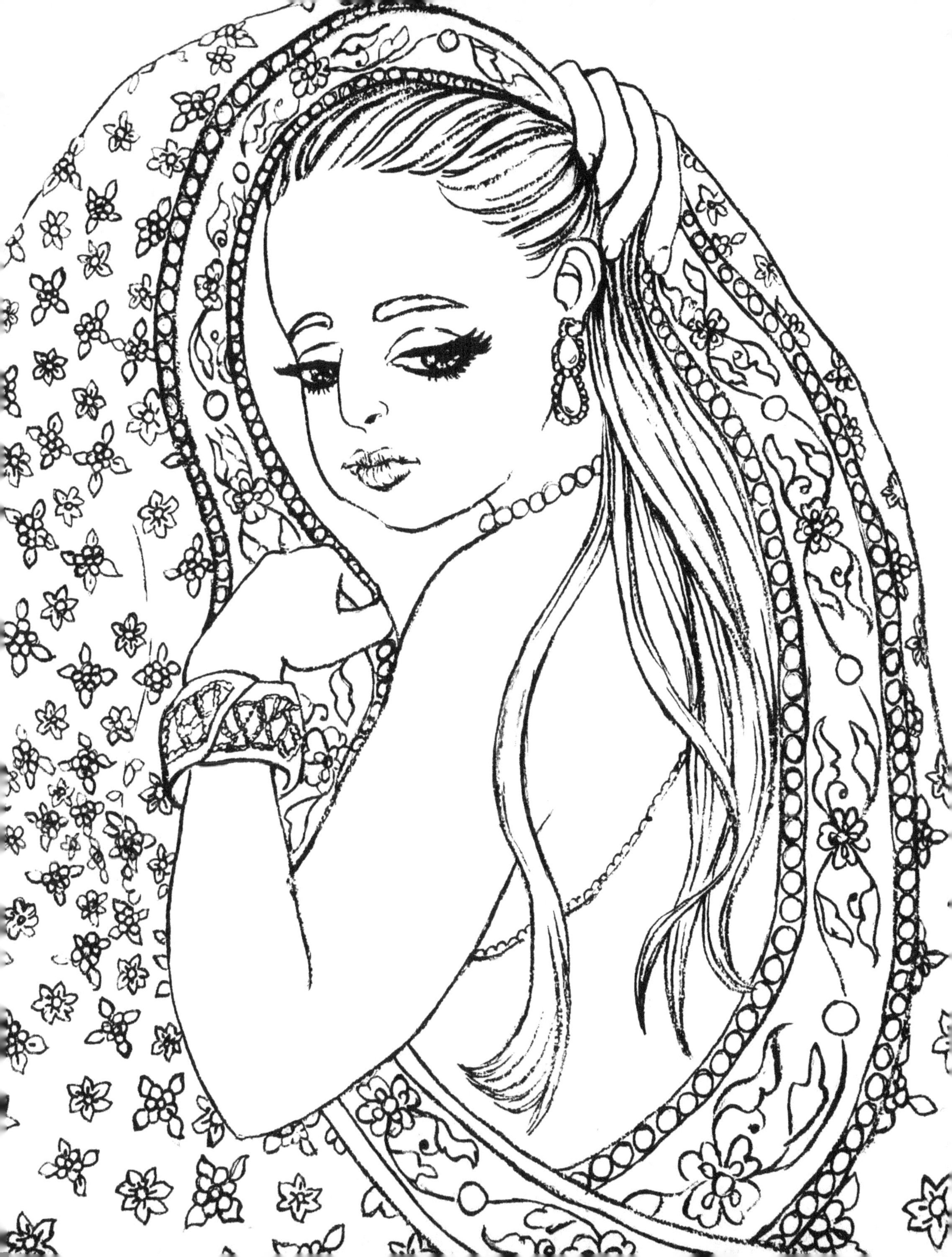

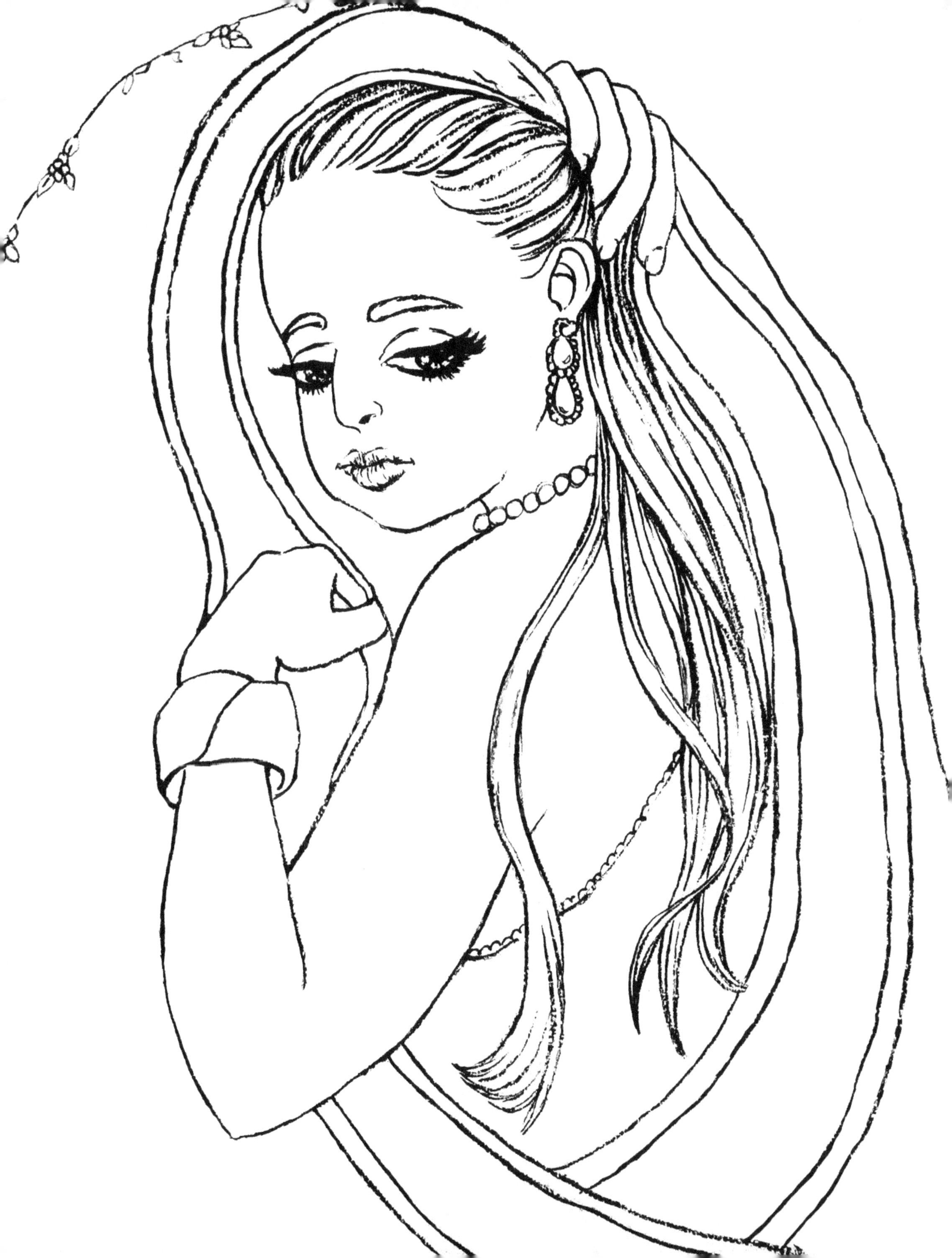

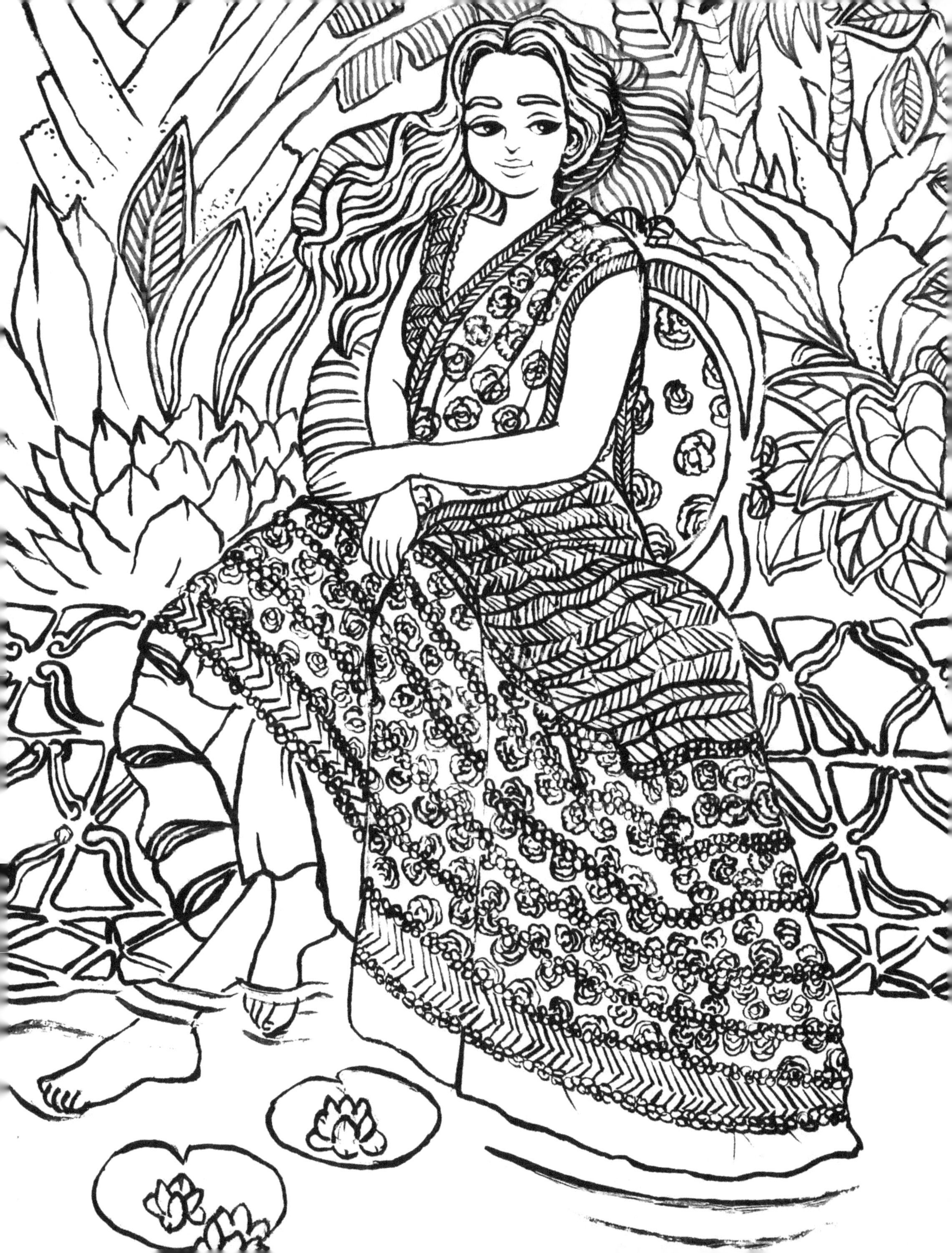

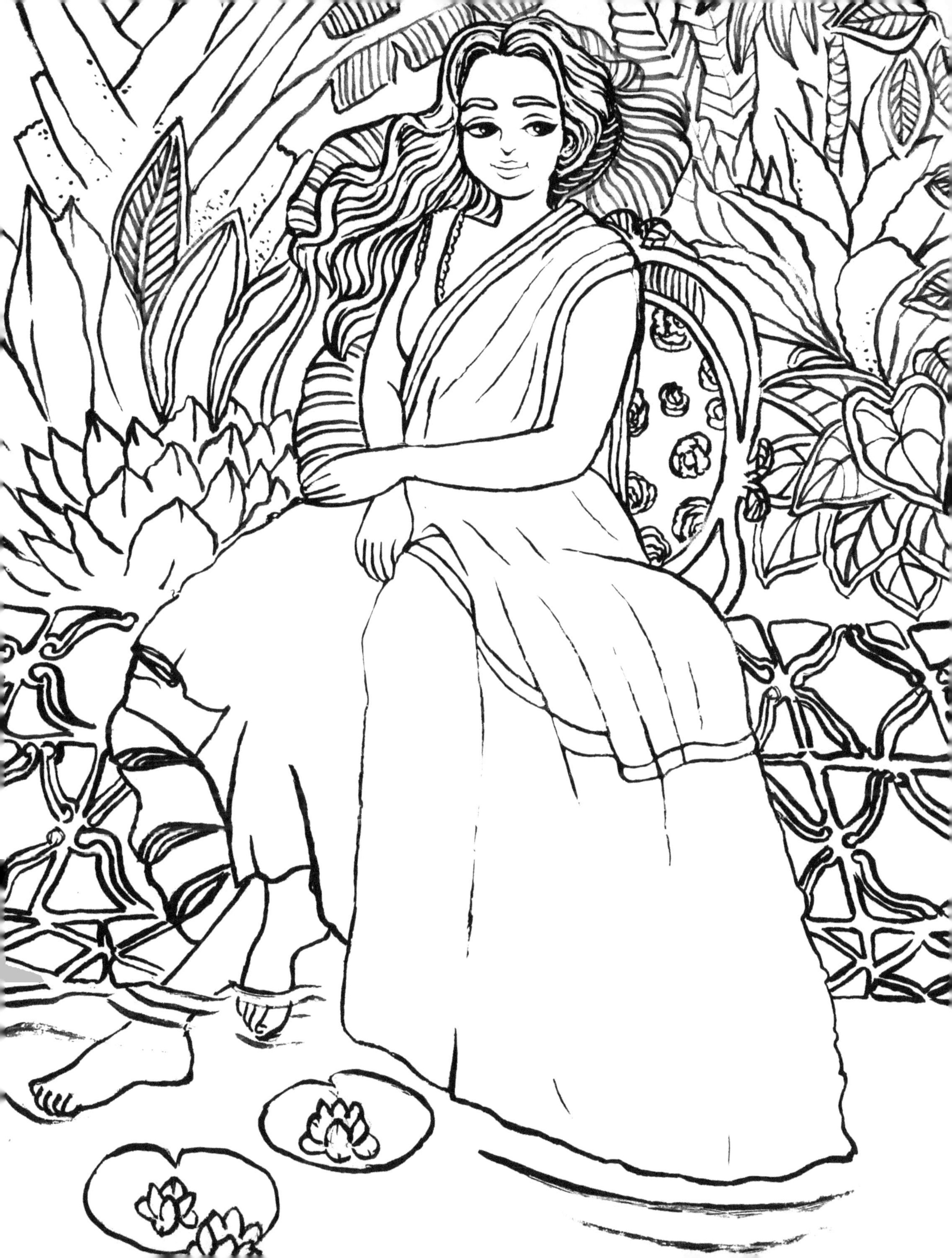

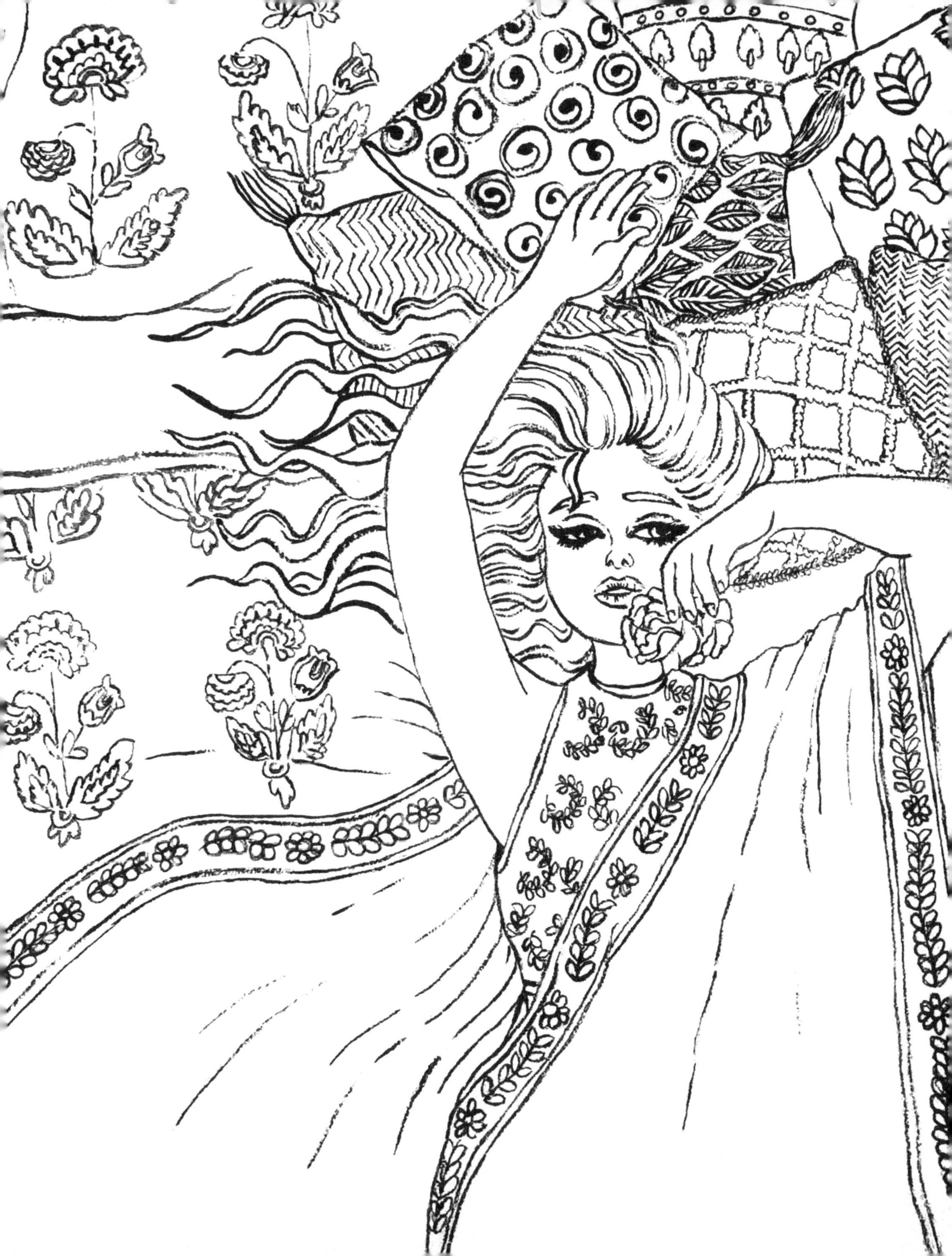

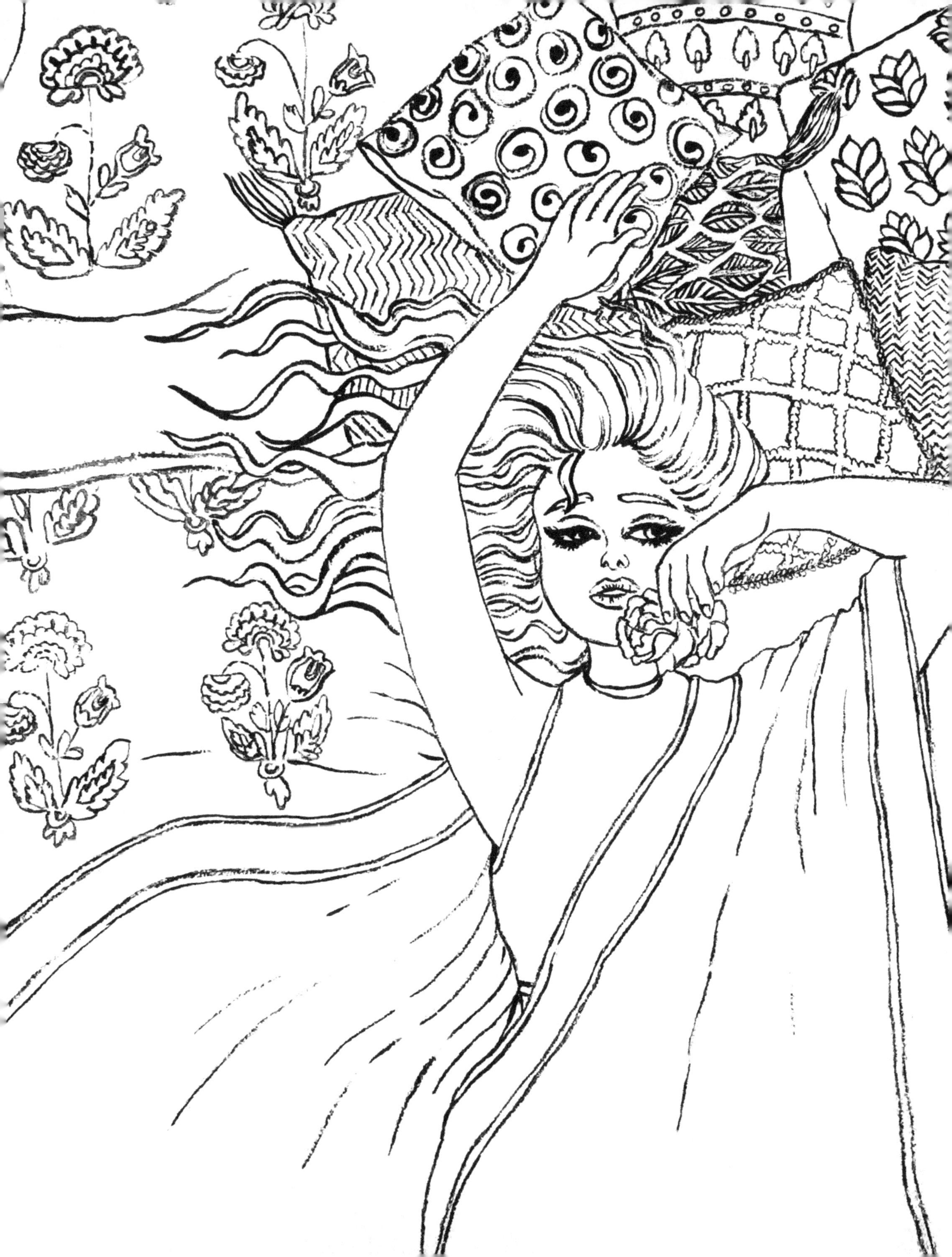

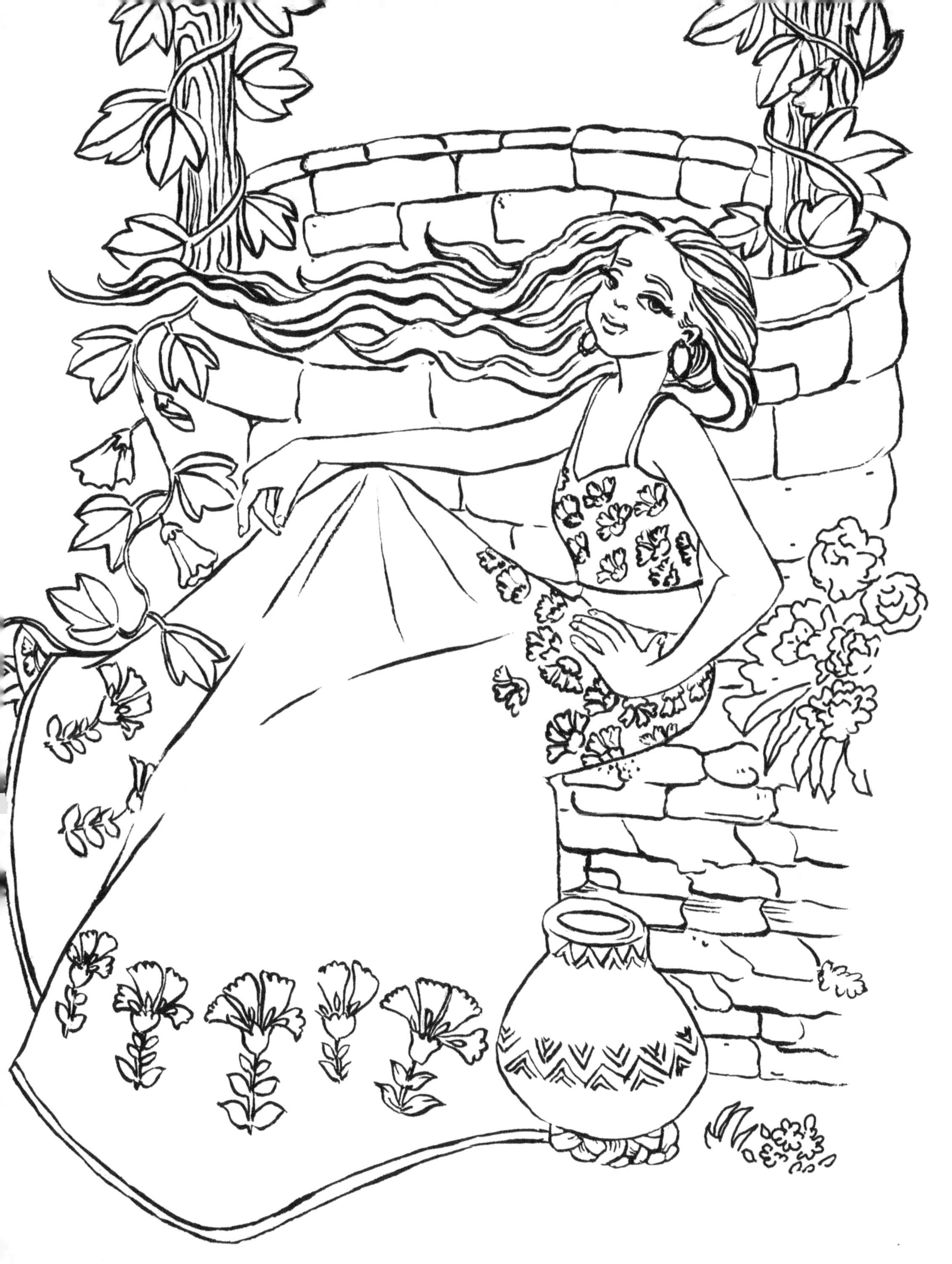

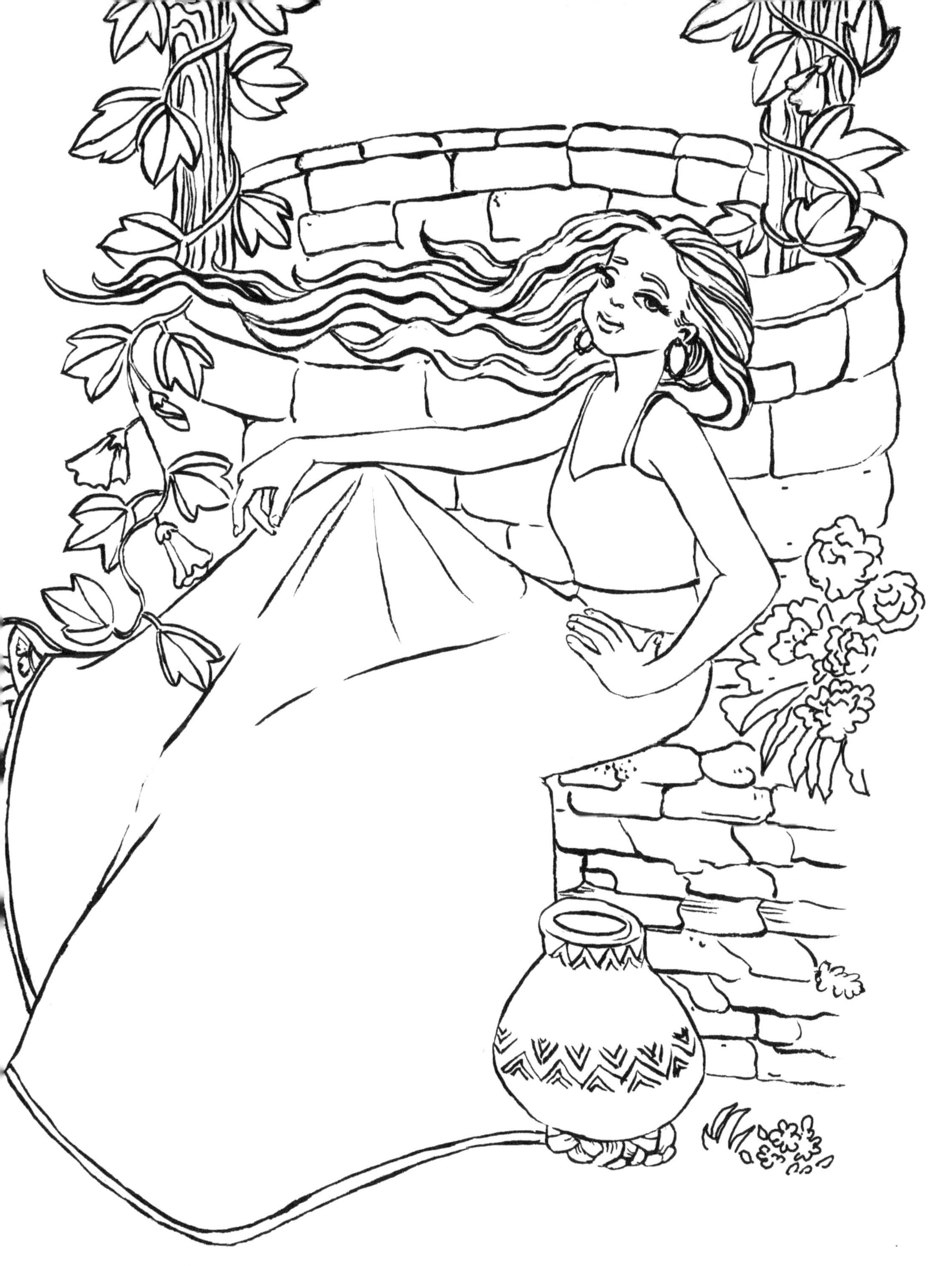

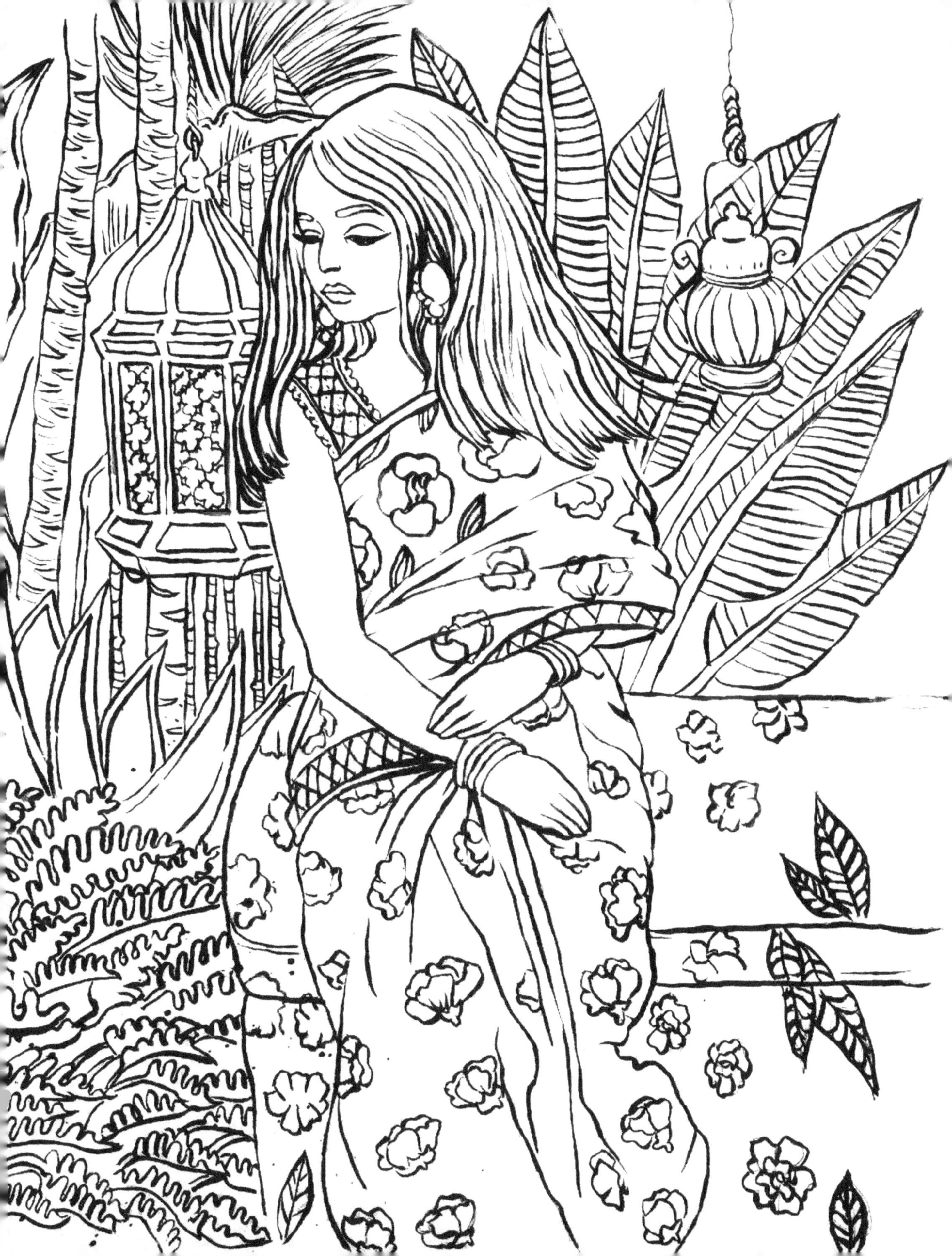

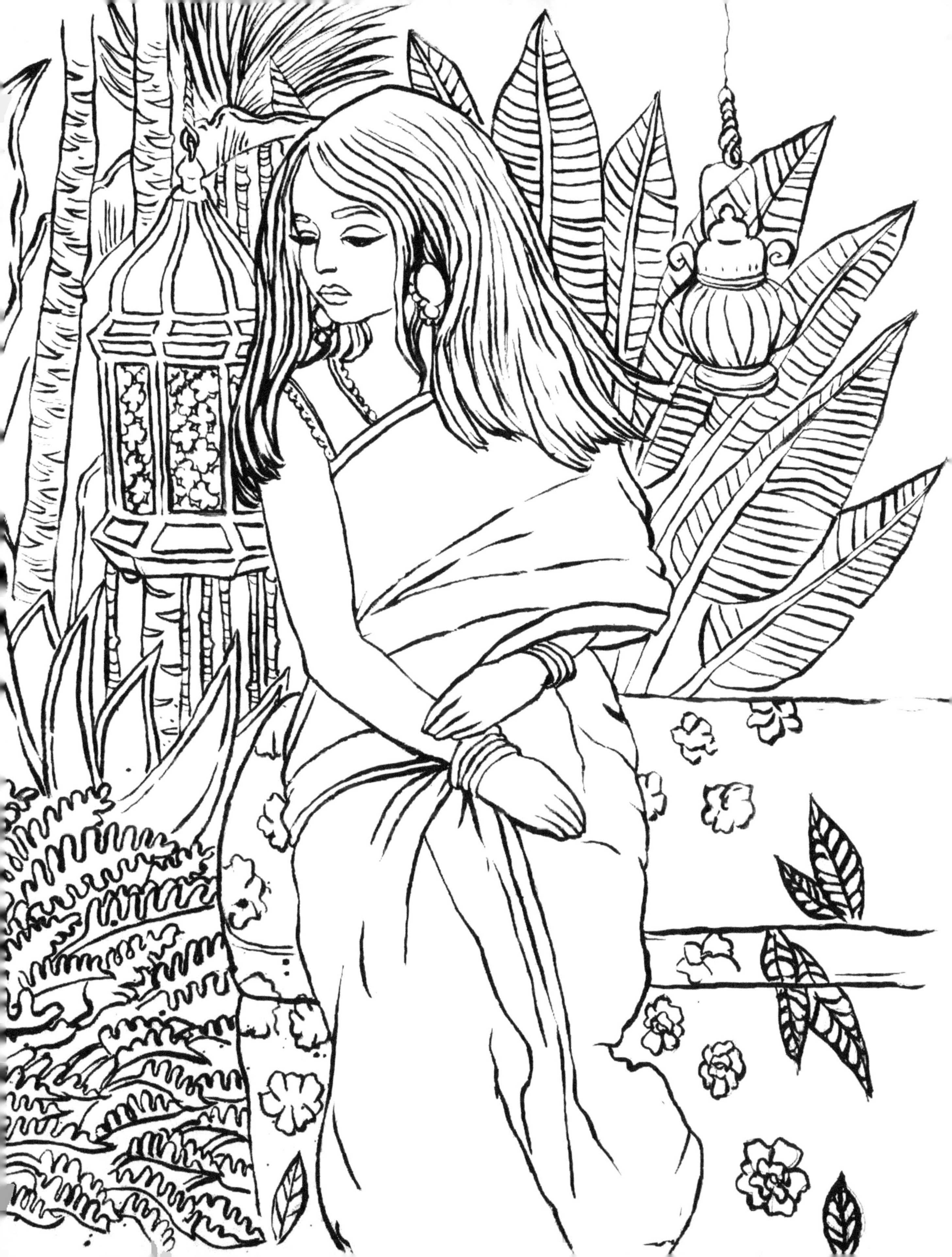

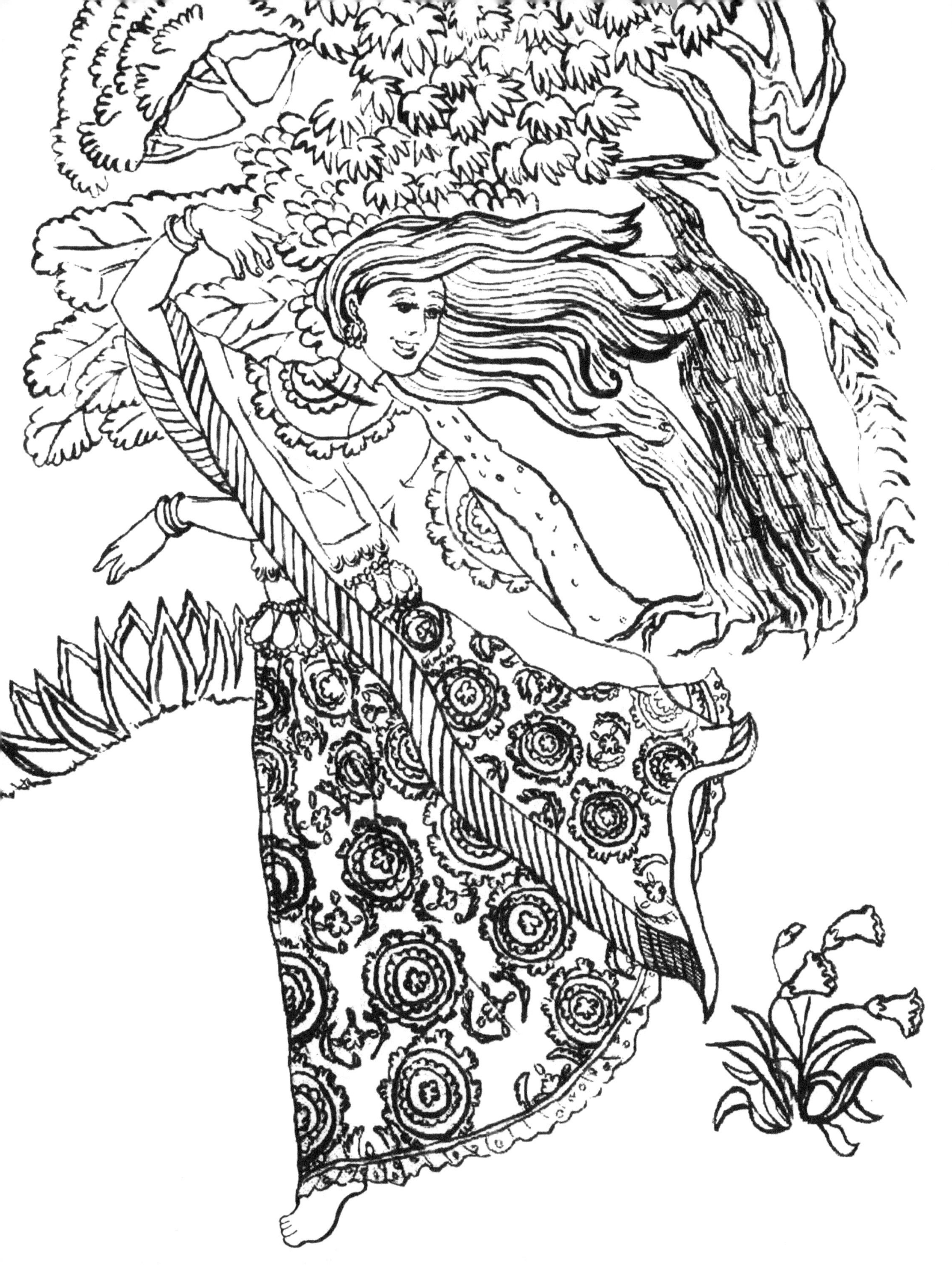

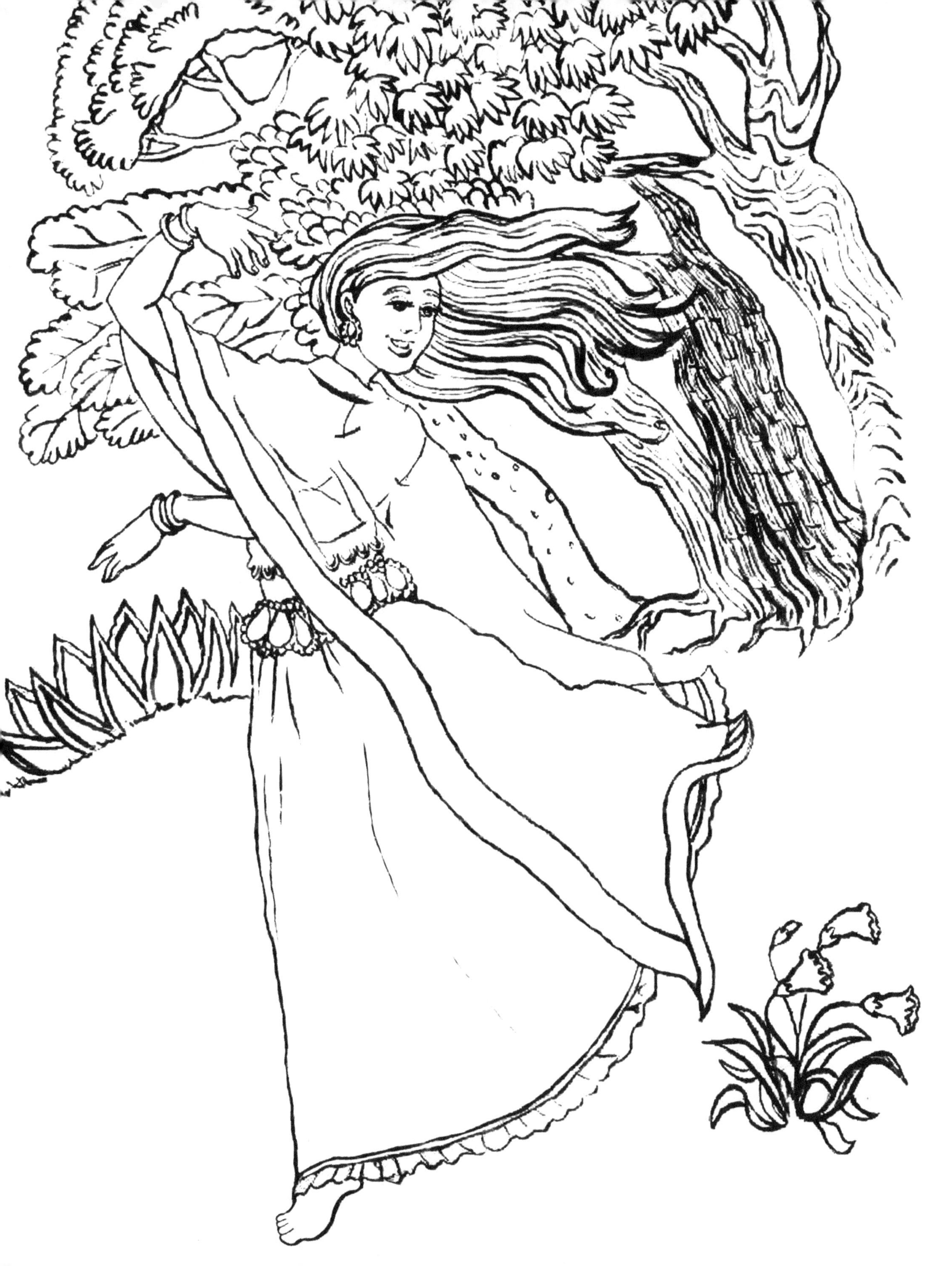

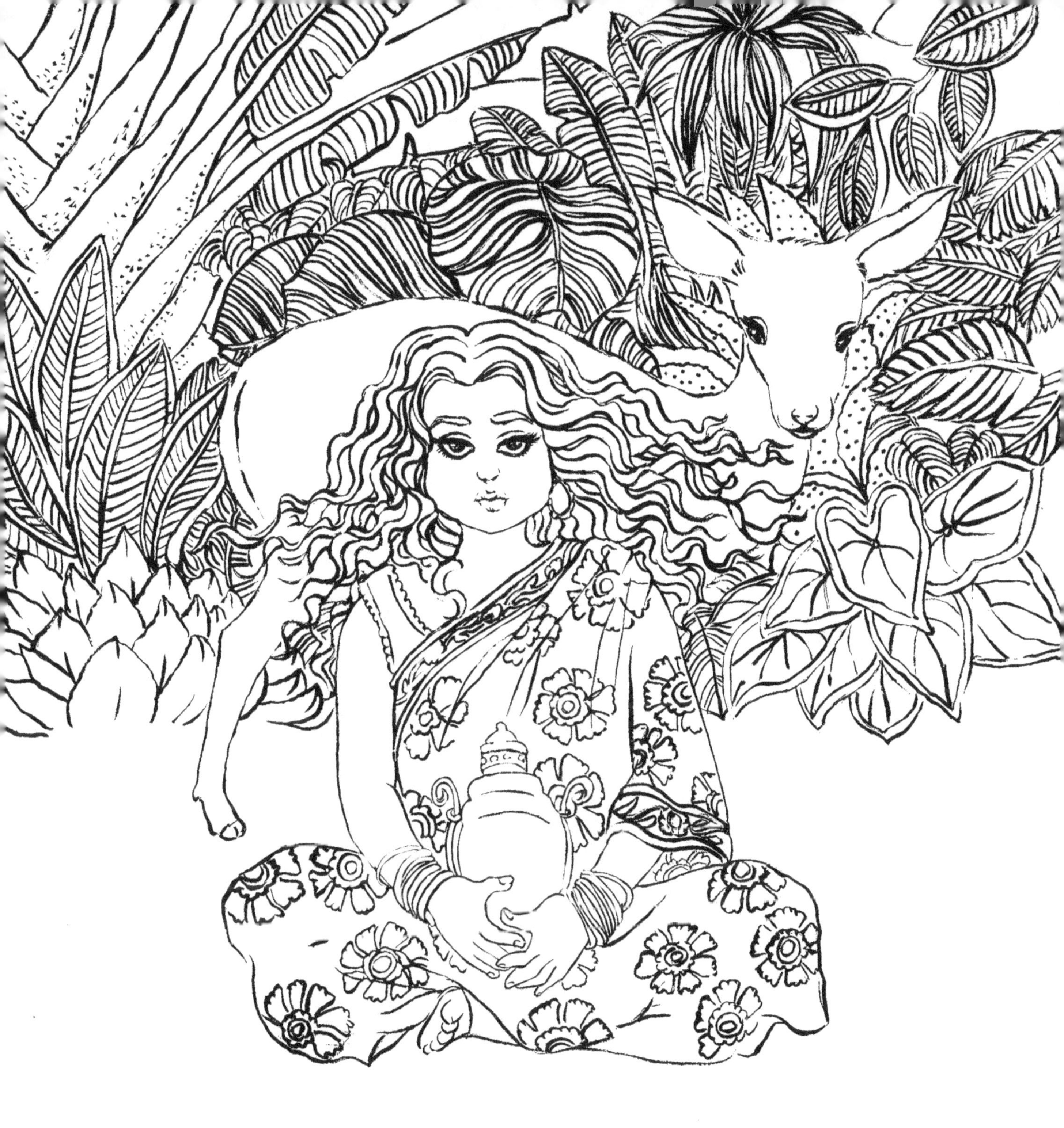

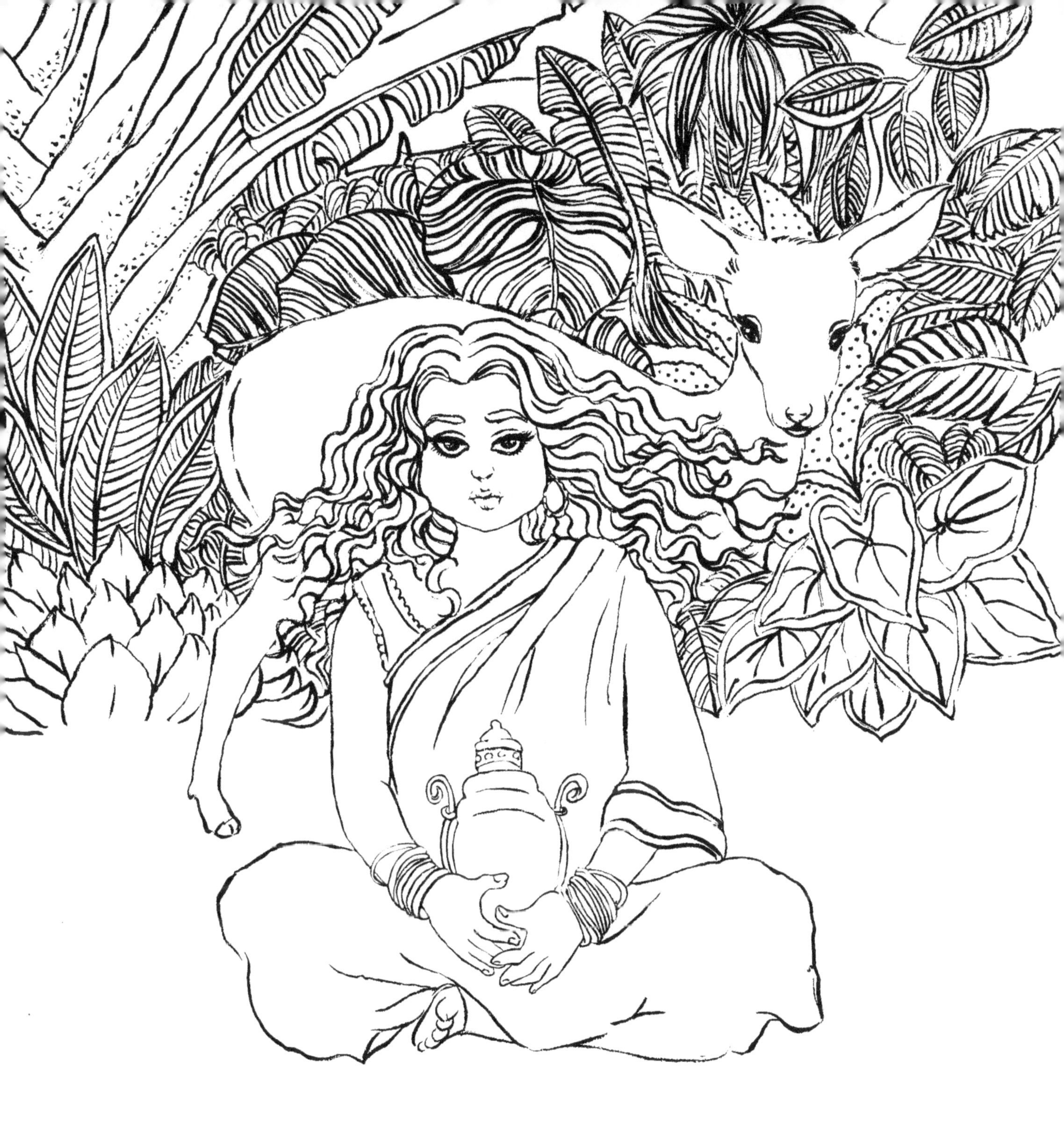

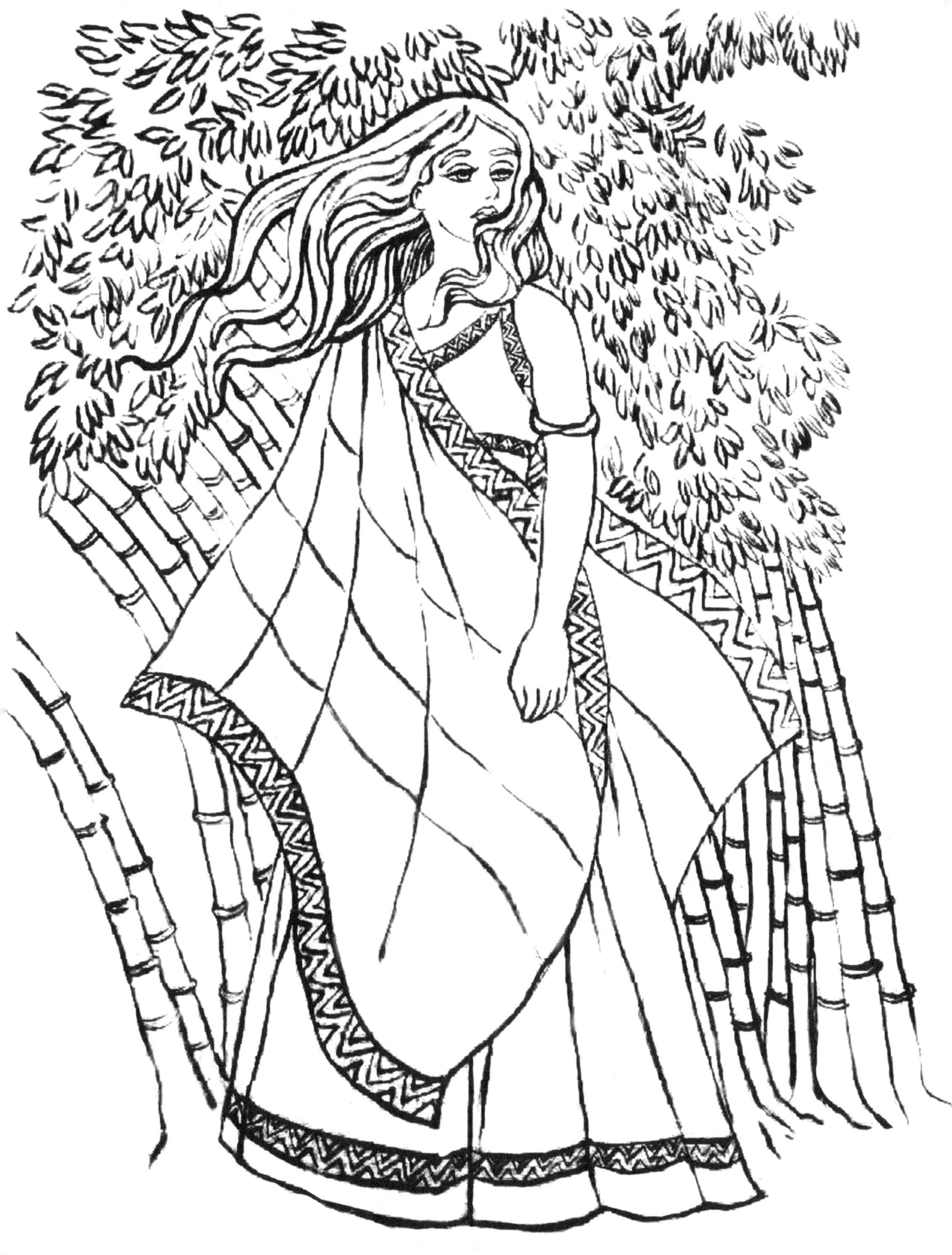

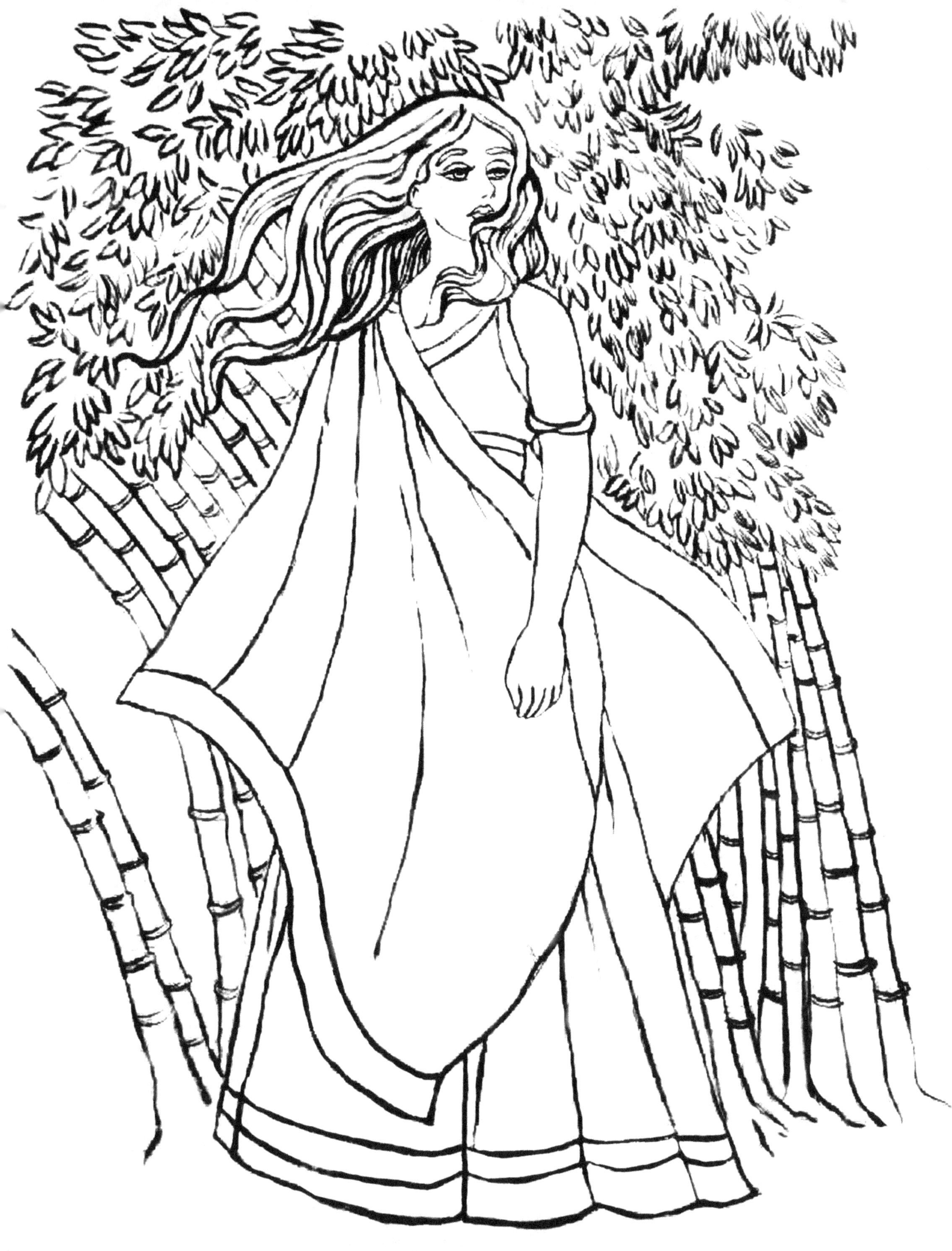

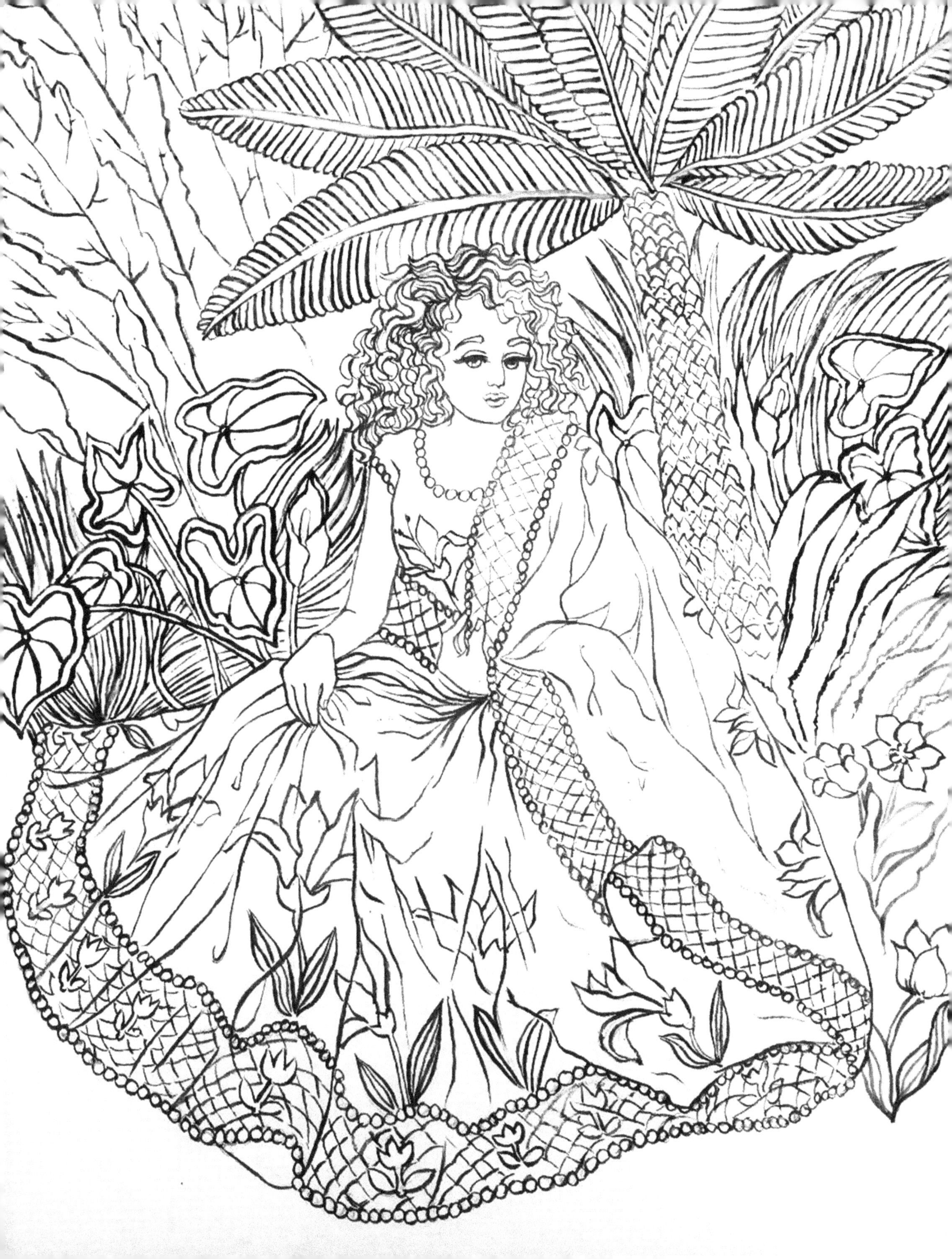

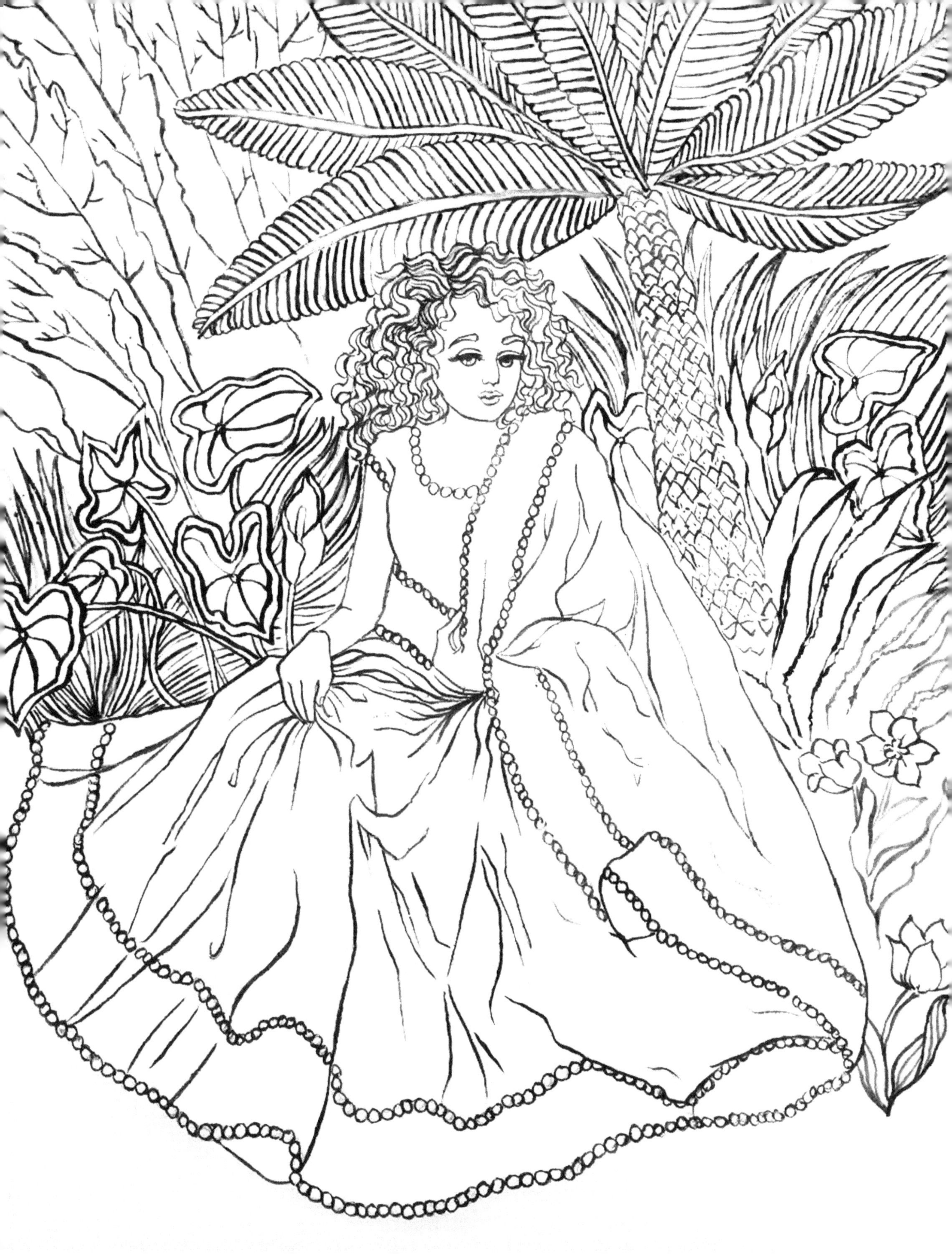

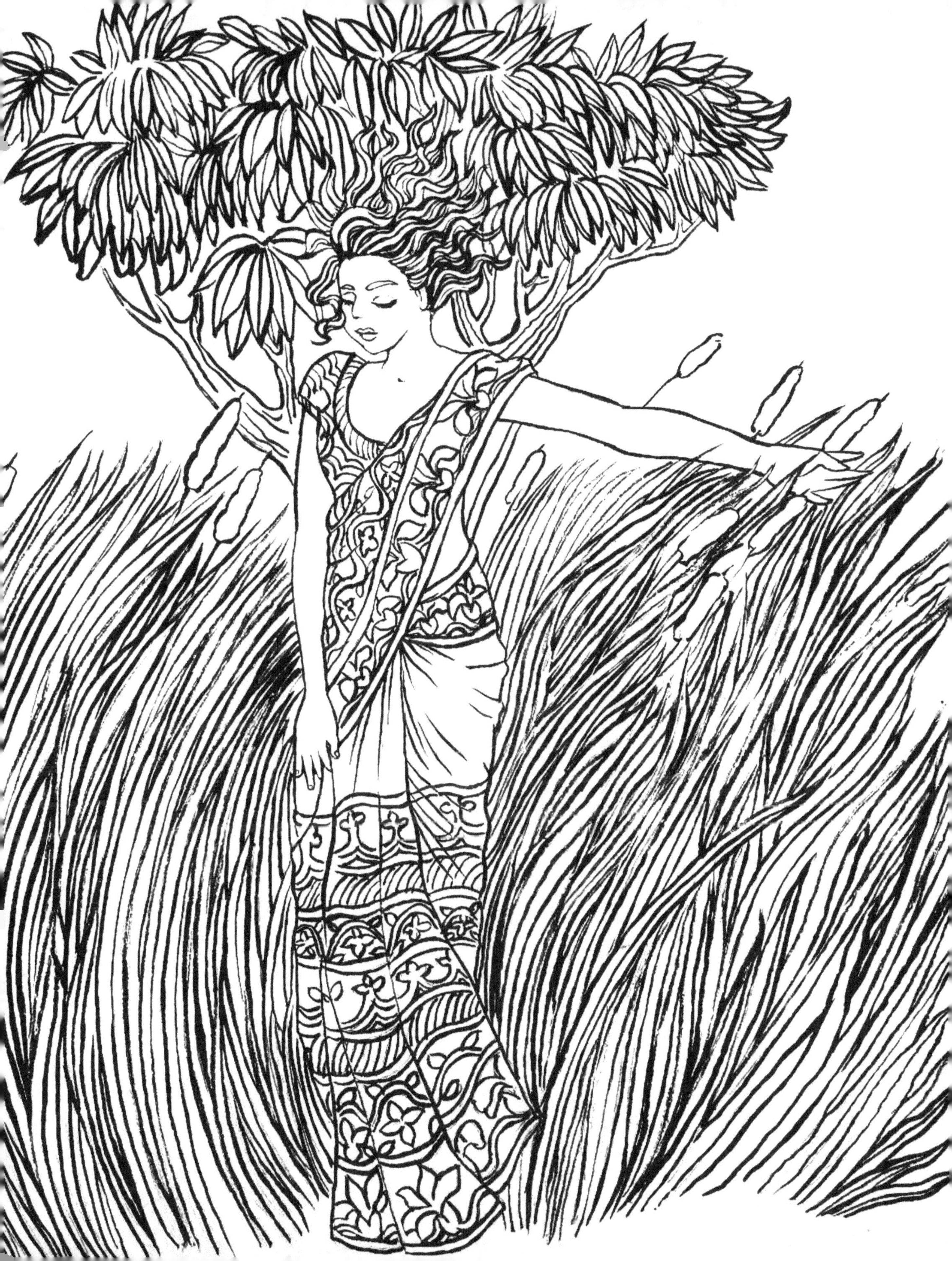

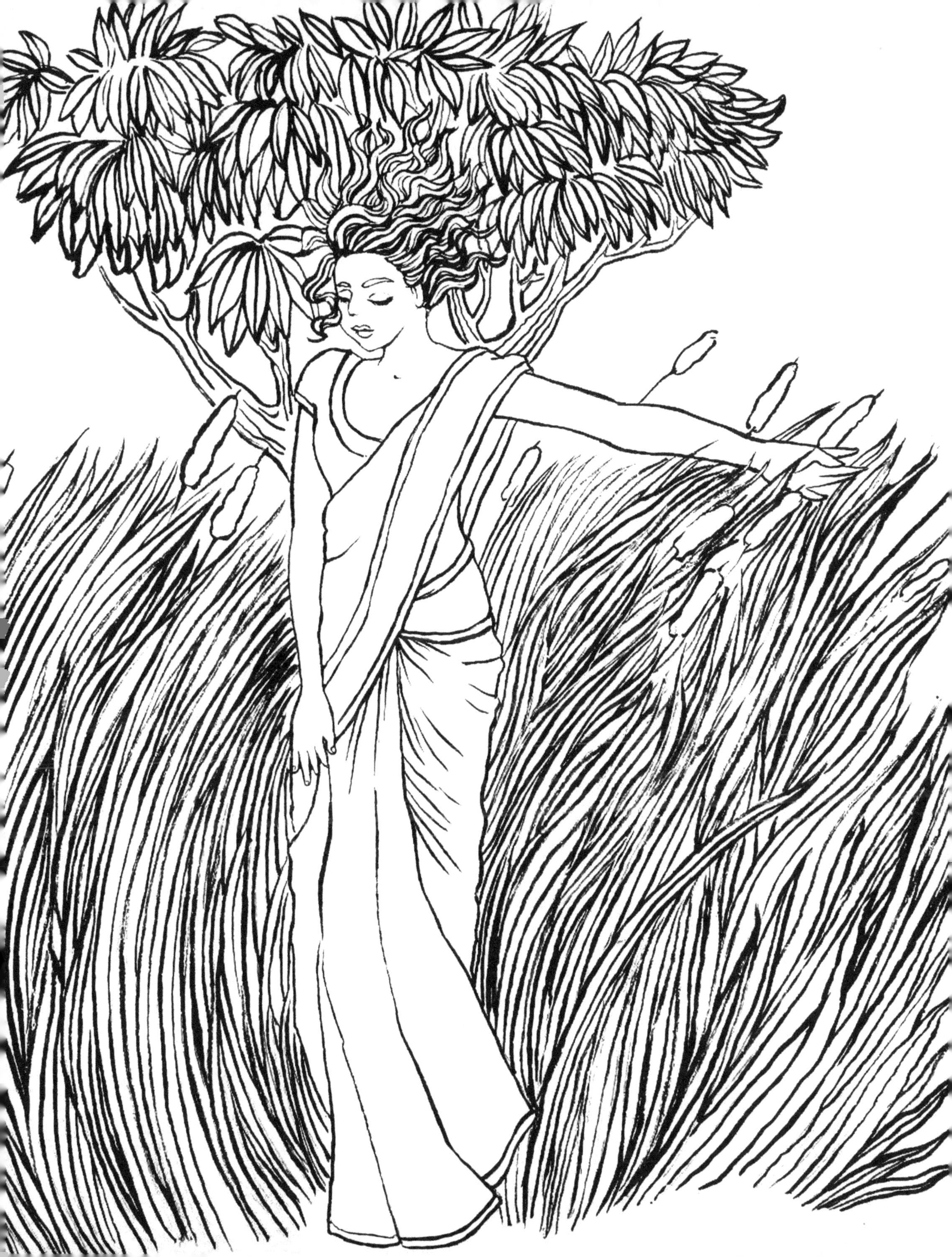

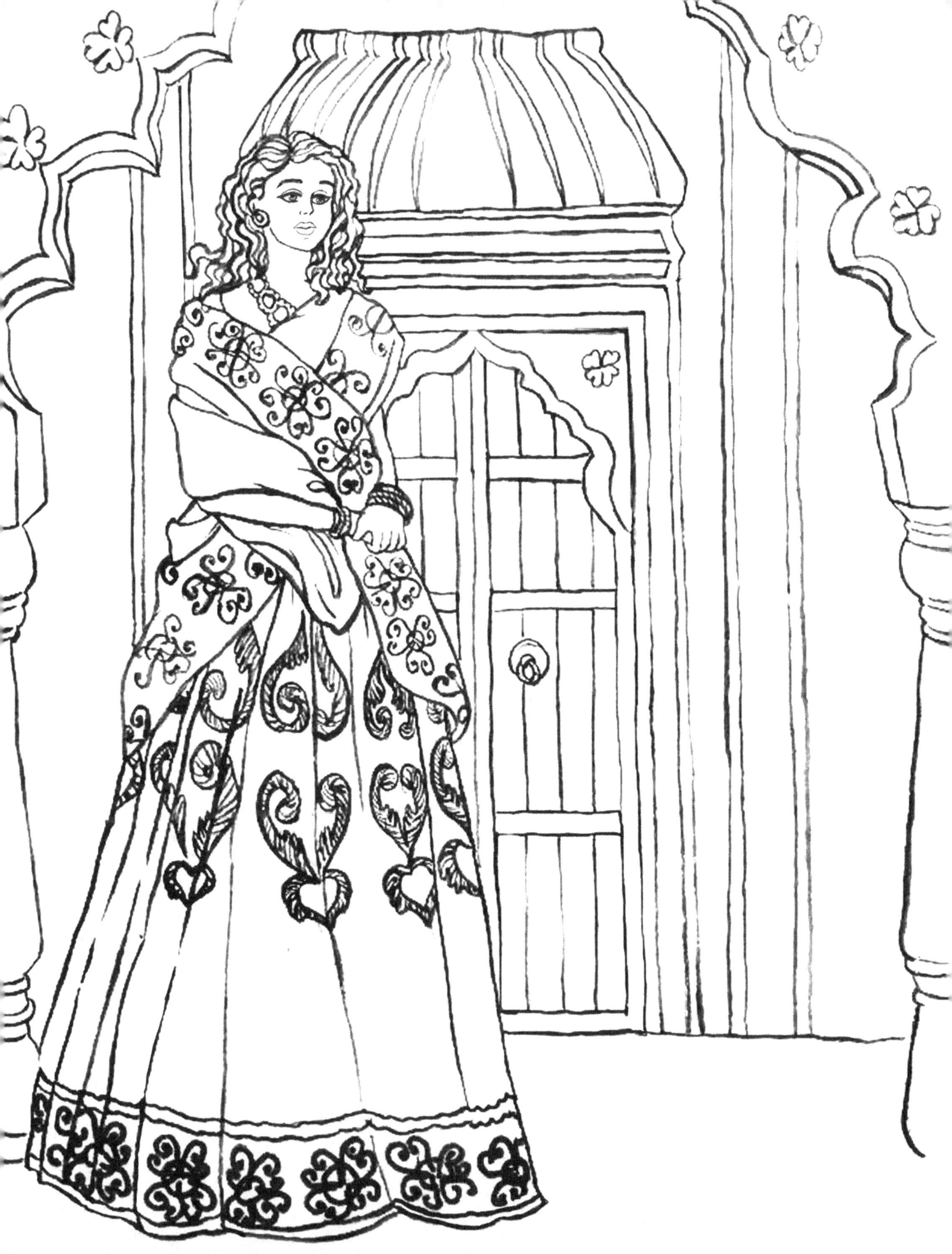

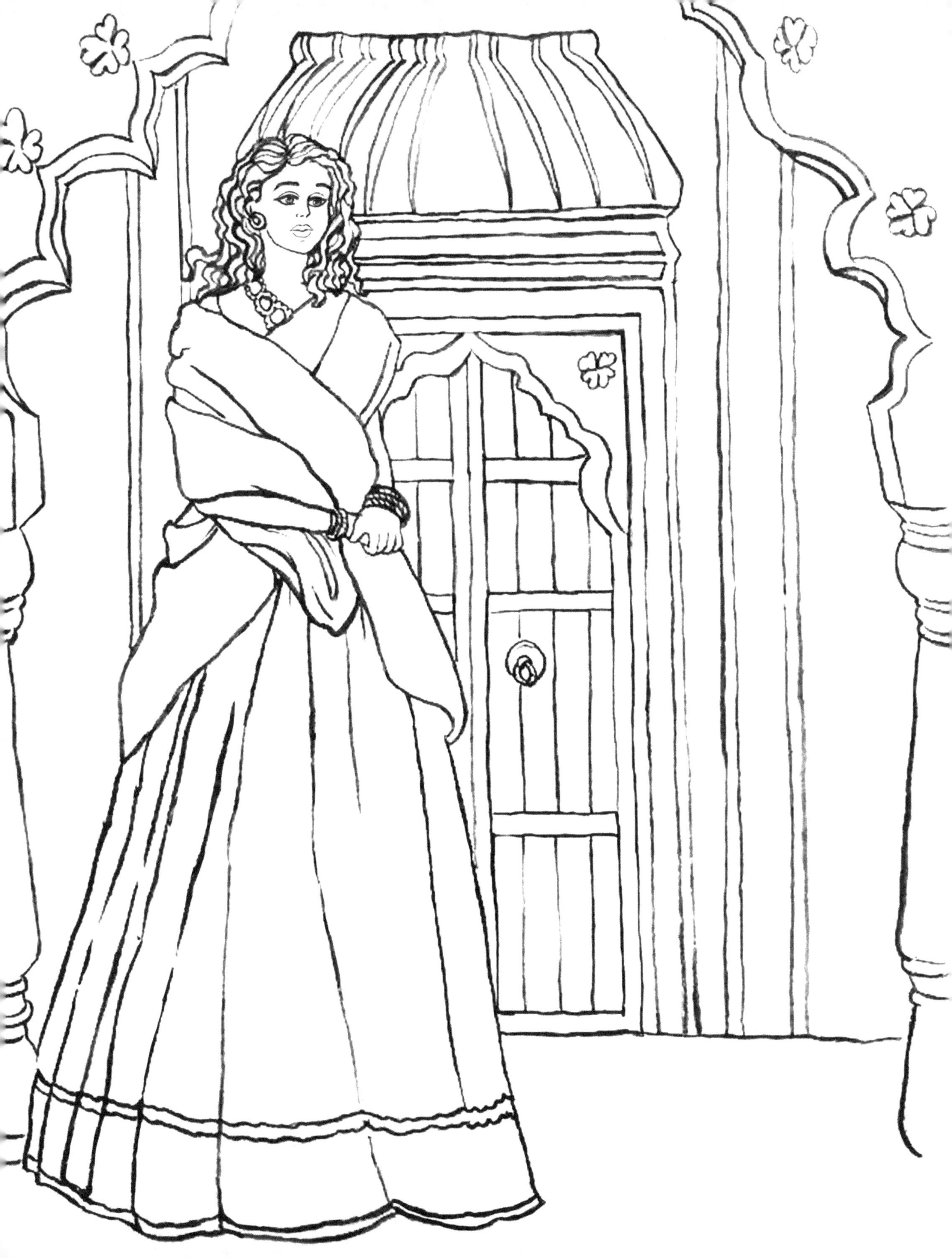

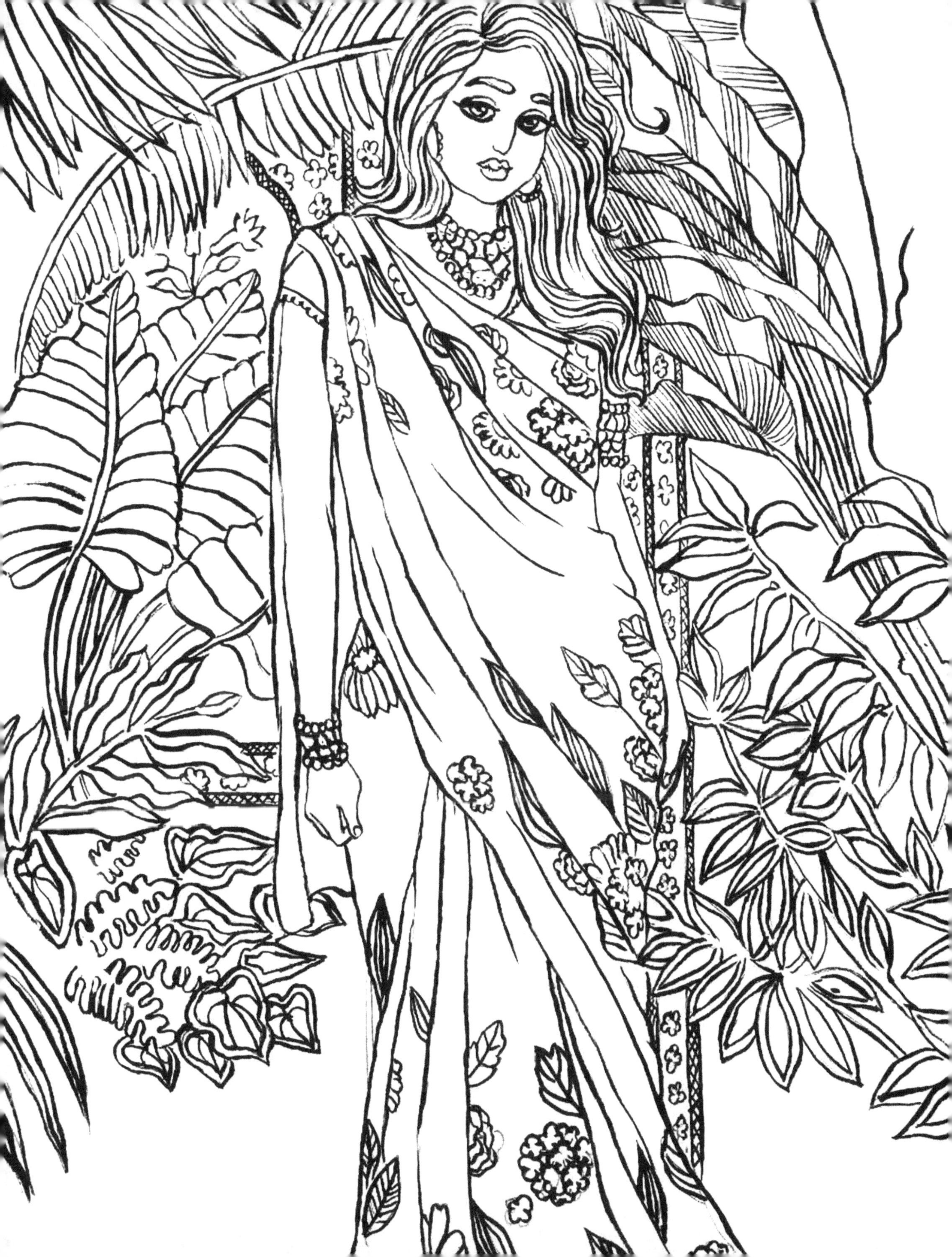

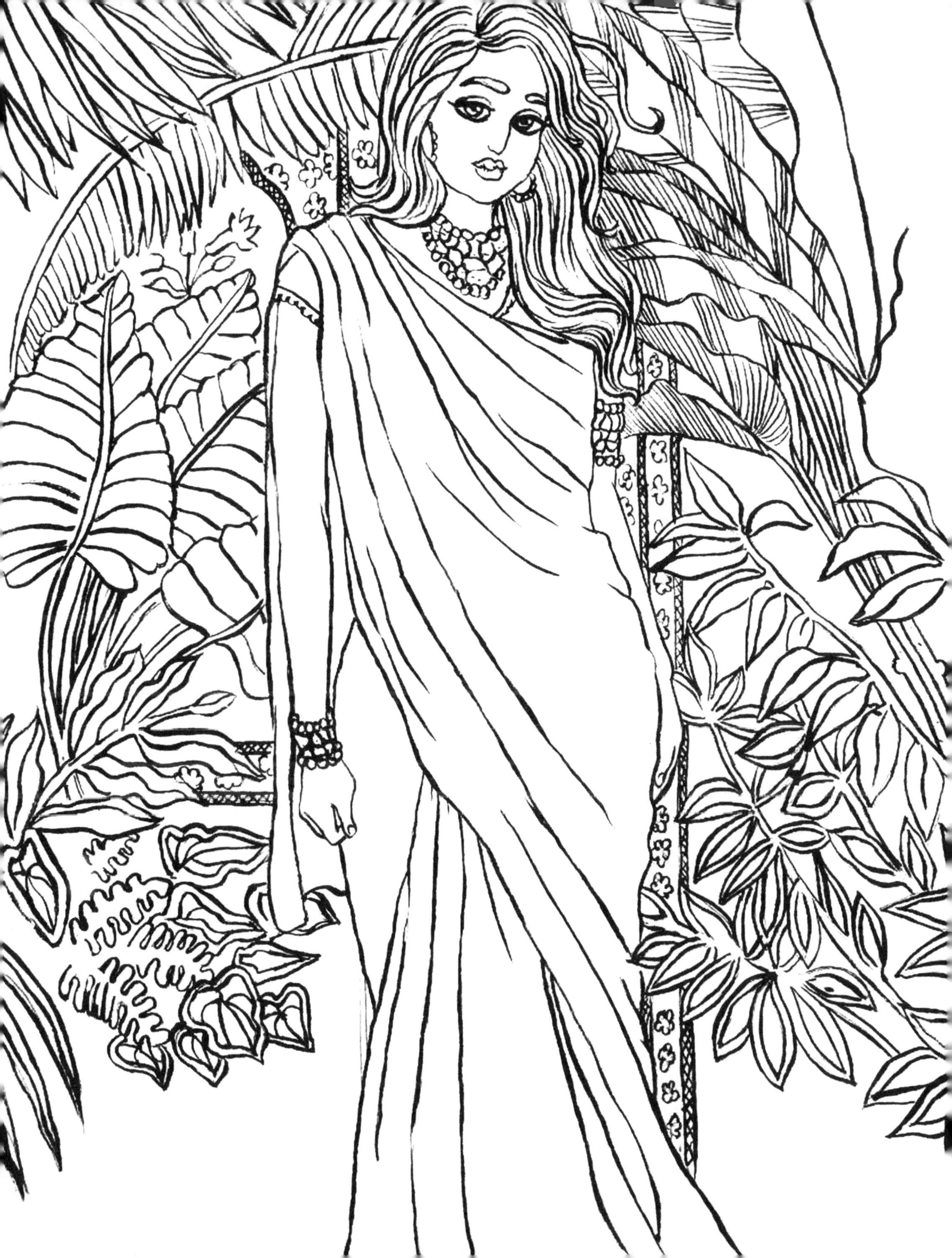